JOHNNY & ME:

The Story of Two Alaskan Children Growing Up Wild

HILDA LUSTER-LINDNER

SUTTON, ALASKA

© 2018 Hilda Luster-Lindner

All rights reserved. Except as permitted under the U.S. Copyright Act of 1976, no part of this publication may be reproduced, distributed, or transmitted in any form or by any means, or stored in a database or retrieval system, without the prior written permission of the publisher.

A special thank you to Harry Buzby, for the use of his family photos.

Relevant Publishers LLC
P.O. Box 505
Sutton, AK 99674

Visit our website at www.relevantpublishers.com

Printed in the United States of America

Luster-Lindner, Hilda
Johnny and Me: The Story of Two Alaskan Children Growing Up Wild / Hilda Luster-Lindner – 1st ed.

ISBN: 978-0-999260548 (paperback)
   978-0-999260555 (ebook)

LCCN: 2018951749

DEDICATION:

For Johnny,

We have always been two peas in a pod.
We shared so many adventures in our lives.
Love you dearly brother.

Hilda

FORWARD

By Harry Buzby

I'm trying to remember the year I first met the Lusters. I think it was somewhere around 1960. Of course, we met through a mutual friend whose family had a homestead in Chickaloon. Hilda was exactly one month older than me, and 'Lil John was not quite a year younger. I spent many days and nights with Hilda and her family, both in Chickaloon and Old Matanuska.

Summers were spent in the Chickaloon area living off the land. We were mischievous, inventive, and camped out a lot, but most of all, we had fun. Reading Hilda's book, <u>Johnny and Me: The Story of Two Alaskan Children Growing Up Wild,</u> brings back so many good memories. When she tells of the shenanigans of yesteryear, it's like it just happened. When she writes about her mother's cooking, I can still smell the moose roast in her oven.

One of my, and I have many, fondest memories of being part of the Luster clan was riding and herding horses from Old Matanuska to Hicks Creek, where we spent just about a whole summer camping on Caribou Creek.

I am a third generation Alaskan. My grandfather came to Alaska in 1886 ahead of the Klondike Gold Rush. I chose to live here after being in Alaska for 68 years, but mostly I cherish the time I got to spend with Hilda and Johnny as children.

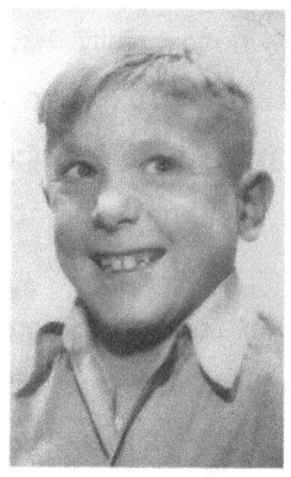 

Harry 7 years old   Harry, 2018

The Story of Two Alaskan Children Growing Up Wild

Mother and the kids with our sled dogs

CHAPTER 1

My lungs hurt from running. I wasn't sure which trail was the one to take me straight home. They all went in the general direction. When I came to the branch in the trail, the very large bear tracks in the mud made my decision an easy one. "I hate bears," I thought as I ran. They always had me up one tree or another. Now it was getting dark, and I had a few more miles to run. An eight-year-old girl would make a

Johnny & Me

nice snack for a bear as large as this one. My older sister had told me many times not to say anything bad about bears, as they laid in the woods and listened to everything that was said about them. If you talked bad about them, they would wait for you the next time you went into the woods. So, I never said anything bad about them aloud, but many things in my head. I didn't think they could hear me thinking, but I could have been wrong.

I came into an open space in the trees. Then I could see the mountain and knew where I was. I just turned off the trail and headed straight for home. In another half hour I made it to the horse pasture and could slow to a walk. I could smell mother was baking bread. Well, she would only have me and the other three little kids to feed as the rest of the kids were camping on the river for one more night. They wanted to finish filling the horse packs with rocks. Rocks could be sold to the jewelry shops in town. I had been sent home to tell mother they would return the next day instead. A slight breeze played with my hair as I walked that last half-mile across the close-cropped pasture. I could see that it was time to move the mares and foals to a new pasture. I could do that in the morning. There would be plenty of time before the pack string returned tomorrow. After all, I only had to catch old Kate, the lead mare. The rest would follow

The Story of Two Alaskan Children Growing Up Wild

her. Kate had a rather ugly colt at her side, kind of dark with a buckskin belly. He had some really long ears too. If I didn't know better, I would think he was a mule. I guessed his father must have been that dark brown stud that belonged to an outfitter, which had stopped by last spring. That colt was no compliment to him. Father wasn't happy that he had been turned loose with our horses. And had hoped that this hadn't happened. Oh well, he would make a gelding.

I was getting pretty hungry, smelling that fresh bread, and broke into a slow run the last hundred yards. I knew mother had churned fresh butter for the big rolls she always made. She would have buttered all the tops, and there was always jam she made from the berries that grew in the hills and valleys. The dogs started barking, heralding my return. No one could come or go around there without everyone knowing about it. I tried to make it to the door before the herd of sled dog pups caught me. They would jump on me and sometimes trip me; then I would get a face licking. Those pups were a very friendly bunch. After making it to the porch without incident, I saw the pups were preoccupied with some bones mother had given them. Father must have come home with meat from a hunt. That was good news, as we had been out of meat for a while and had to rely on the chicken's mother raised. Now, I like

Johnny & Me

chicken as much as the next person, but we had been eating chicken for over two months with only some trout from the lake now and then on our menu. And those chickens weren't that big to feed eight children. Bear would be a great change. The opened door brought the wonderful smell of a roast still in the oven. Now that mother had bear-lard, she would bake pies. It only got better. Mother asked where the others were. I told her as I looked into the pots on the stove.

My brother, Johnny, must have gone fiddlehead fern picking. There was a pot of steamed fiddlehead ferns swimming in fresh churned butter. I could see dinner was ready to put on the table. The little girls had set the table. They were now removing four of the place settings. I started to sit at the table, but jumped up when mother cleared her throat. Hands and face needed attention. Shortly I was back at the table with a shining clean face and hands. I really was hungry. We all waited while mother said our dinner prayer. Asking for safety for the absent children and father, whom went back to the mountains on another bear hunt. I was hoping mother wouldn't spend too much time on the prayer, as my stomach was beginning to rumble with anticipation of soon being filled. My hand was on a roll as mother finished the amen. I saw the raised eyebrow but ignored it and set to

The Story of Two Alaskan Children Growing Up Wild

my dinner with gusto. Mother only smiled.

Mother insisted on eating like town folk ever since someone in town gave her a set of fancy glass dishes. I would sure be glad when they were all broken. Maybe we would go back to eating natural like before. Why mother had even sewn a tablecloth to cover the old board table that father had made. Although that table didn't look half bad, the way mother scrubbed and oiled it you would have thought it was worth a million dollars.

Mother told us that just because we lived in the mountains didn't mean we had to be savages. I kind of preferred being a little savage myself. All that hair combing and ear washing just didn't appeal to me. After all, the only running water we had was in a creek running past the house. That creek wasn't all that close and carrying buckets to fill the reservoir wasn't that much fun. Just think how much water we could save carrying, if mother didn't have to wash everything all the time. We could save a lot of water if we didn't have to fill that bathtub on Saturday too. I didn't think a little dirt hurt anything. Mother on the other hand was always checking behind our ears and the back of our neck. Lucky for me, I chewed my fingernails. There was no place for dirt. Mother always checked there too.

My sleeping bag felt extra nice tonight, as I was

pretty worn out and that wonderful dinner just knocked me out. Father had provided each of us with a down, army sleeping bag. I think he got them from soldiers in trade for pack trips. We had no idea what sheets were, never having seen any. Also look at the water that saved, you never washed a down sleeping bag. Just hung it on the line once or twice a year to air out. The only washing they ever got was if one of the packhorses tripped in a river crossing. But none of that was ever my concern. It was just cozy and warm, cuddled up with one of my precious books for a pillow.

The morning was just peaking over Castle Mountain when I walked into the pasture to get old Kate. She always seemed happy to be with people and trotted up to nuzzle my hand in hopes of a treat. With the gate already opened, I just climbed up and took a turn around the pasture to collect the rest of the mares. Then I headed out to the lower fields. Kate was the bell mare; so all the others would follow her when they heard the bell moving. It made for an easy job. The bell not only kept the horses together. It also kept the bears away from the horses. It helped find the herd as well. The cows had bells also.

After moving the horses I went to sit on the hillside. It was nice to watch the valley come alive in the morning. The

The Story of Two Alaskan Children Growing Up Wild

morning sun dappled the deep moss under the spruce trees. It was softer than any Persian rug I had ever read about. Though I had not ever been on a carpet of any kind. The only wall to wall we had ever known was maybe dogs. Our floors were boards. Sometimes in winter we put a saddle blanket on the floor next to our beds. But saddle blankets were valuable, and we tried to keep them in good condition. They were cleaned and shook out more often than our sleeping bags.

My morning daydreams were interrupted when I heard my brother Johnny calling me. I had forgotten I promised I would go fishing with him this morning. My brother was small and skinny. Kind of a runt you might say. I wasn't much bigger, but I was a girl and almost a year older. Looking down the hill, Johnny could be seen carrying two fishing poles and a burlap bag, following behind was Big Yella, a very large sled dog. Bringing Big Yella was a good idea, as he didn't mind riding on the pontoon raft and was good bear protection. Big Yella was one of only a few dogs we had ever had that could be left off a chain and not have to worry about him killing half the livestock or all of mother's chickens. That dog was the best kid protector and friend ever. He was also one of father's best sled and pack dogs. We all loved him.

Johnny & Me

After joining Johnny, we headed for the lake to spend the morning fishing and poling the raft around the lake. Johnny had brought two large buns filled with jam. We finished those off, saving a bite for Big Yella, before climbing onto the raft. Big Yella hopped on board and found his usual place to lie down and watch us fish. The only way he ever moved was if one of us tripped over him, and that could happen when you had a good size fish on the line.

We could pole out about one hundred and fifty feet before it was to deep to reach the bottom. The poles were long to compensate for the three feet of mud on the bottom. Getting back to shore was not a problem as the raft would always drift back, if not anchored. There was a cement filled lard can with an eyebolt attached to a long rope that served as an anchor.

The sun warmed raft and pine filled breeze soon made us sleepy. With a full stringer of land locked silver salmon tied to the raft, we both fell asleep next to Big Yella. We woke to see a cow moose mostly submerged in the lake eating water plants. The water ran off her head and dripped from her ears as she raised her head from the water to breath. On the shore were two red twin calves waiting for her to feed. They soon curled up in a patch of weeds near a log and became almost invisible. We watched them for an

The Story of Two Alaskan Children Growing Up Wild

hour then pulled anchor and let the raft drift toward shore, poling now and then to keep a good distance from the moose family. A mother moose can be very dangerous. We had an older friend that was trampled just a week earlier. He was trying to photograph her calves. Although he carried a handgun, he wouldn't shoot that cow because he didn't want to orphan her calves. He said she was just trying to protect her babies. He got away by rolling under some felled trees. He was a lucky man. We didn't want to get ourselves in that same position, although we did have Big Yella to help us.

After putting our fish in the burlap bag, we tied it on Big Yella's back for our walk home. We walked home leaving two sets of small bare foot tracks and one set of large dog tracks in the deep dust of the trail. Ahead of us in the trail was a spruce hen flopping around and dragging one wing. We ignored her and started peeking under the cranberry bushes beside the trail. Sure enough huddled as flat as they could get were eight or nine small striped balls of fluff. They were hard to see among the dead leaves and grass. If not for the mother's efforts to lure us away, we would never have discovered them. We moved away after a quick peek so that the mother could come back for them. Laughing at the hen, we headed towards home.

Johnny & Me

It was not yet noon when we reached the house. Already the big girls were back with the pack string. After giving mother the fish, we were enlisted to help put the horses back in a pasture. I am sure the girls were tired and hungry. Mother was busy fixing a lunch for everyone. Thick slices of bear roast on equally thick slices of fresh bread. Cups of milk that were icy cold from chilling in the spring box, to wash down the sandwiches. Mother even had a few scraps that she gave to Big Yella.

The afternoon was spent climbing in our willow tree, which had become a sailing ship. The tallest limbs we could climb were the sail rigging, where we watched for pirates. Later in the day, the tree became a tree house and home to Tarzan. Under the tree were lions and elephants, which happened to resemble sled dogs and horses. We stayed in the tree until the pygmy tribe was sighted. Then we had to come down for dinner, as the pygmy tribe demanded that mother had sent them out to get us. Besides, we had dogs and chickens to feed and eggs to gather. We made a game of that too. Although going into the chicken yard was a risk if you didn't watch out for the geese. They would bite and hold on, then beat you with their wings. We carried a good-sized stick to ward them off, but that didn't always work. We both had pinch marks on our backsides and bruises on

The Story of Two Alaskan Children Growing Up Wild

our arms and legs from failed encounters with those geese. I would be happy to see them served up for Christmas dinner. I think that would be when I liked them best. I am sure Johnny felt the same. I hoped mother would get turkeys next year for holiday dinners. Or maybe we could just eat one of the pigs. Father always made good ham in the smoke house.

We had no trouble with the geese this time, as they were behind the chicken house. When we locked up the chickens for the night we left the geese out. That way we never had to deal with them, but if mother found out, we would be in it up to our ears. She wanted those geese for us to eat, not the coyotes. With plenty of daylight this time of year, I spent time reading a western novel that I had found in an old bus. I loved to escape into the worlds of books. Learning to read was one of the greatest things that had happened in my life. Mother and father didn't hold the same opinion. They were sure I was wasting time when I could be doing something useful. But to me, it was useful. I read everything I could find. I even read the encyclopedias cover to cover. Which didn't help me with my sisters, as I always had an answer for everything. Well to be quite frank, it didn't please father much either. I did have a tendency to share my answers with everyone, whether they wanted to hear

Johnny & Me

them or not. It took me many years to curb that habit. It still isn't completely cured.

But on this night, I was happy to have a western novel to escape in to. The sun doesn't quite go down in midsummer, and even though it was still technically spring, it stayed light far into the evening. I woke to find my book against my cheek where it had fallen when sleep had overtaken me. I dressed quickly so I could meet the morning before anyone else woke. After tucking the book under my sleeping bag so father wouldn't find it, I quietly moved past the other bunks to the door. Johnny raised his head and grinned at me. He also slid out of his sleeping bag to join me. When we were away from the house, we made plans for the day. If we could get our ponies and leave before anyone got up, we would have the whole day for ourselves. We stopped at the meat shed and grabbed a few pieces of jerky off the line. Our next stop was the saddle shed for a couple of bridles. Then we were gone. The ponies were well away from the house, and we rode them out the back gate to avoid being seen. We galloped into the morning.

That was a great day spent mostly at the lower lake catching frogs and small bullhead fish. There were plenty of small flat rocks for skipping and bigger ones for throwing. The loons honored us with their haunting calls. Other

The Story of Two Alaskan Children Growing Up Wild

waterfowl could also be seen swimming, followed by small trains of their young. The mother swan sailed across the lake carrying some of her babies on her back, while the others bobbed behind. Even the muskrats continued their work and paid us no mind. When it was near dinnertime, we picked some water lilies for mother and headed home. No one had missed us that day, and mother seemed pleased to get the lilies. She floated them in a bowl on the table. Mother had made a stew, thick with meat and potatoes. She also made boiled dandelion greens with vinegar. Of course, we had fresh baked bread with freshly churned butter.

    After dinner mother sent the four younger children out to weed in her garden and had the older girls wash the dishes. It was only fair for us to do something as we had skipped work all day. I think we spent more time eating the baby carrots and onions than weeding to be honest. But mother had stayed us from eating too many, as we were full from dinner. After about an hour of being in the garden, we got side tracked and went to catching some baby rabbits that were in the weeds at the end of the garden. We caught three or four and went to put them back in some hutches in the chicken yard. At least mother would be happy, they weren't eating her garden. She hadn't been to happy when one of the rabbits had gotten out. Apparently it had been a

Johnny & Me

pregnant doe. Rabbits can ruin a garden in a hurry. Besides, we had them to raise fryers. Father had traded for a buck and two does. Now we had several does and two bucks. We would catch the rest of the rabbits now that we knew where they were. Just wait for the mother to go down the hole and then cover it. Since she had two entrances you just dug out the other hole and reached in and grabbed them. Anyway, that was how we caught them. I think that rabbit was the first to grace the table, as mother was mad at it for eating some of her garden. Really she didn't eat much, but that was our winter stores, I guess.

That evening mother read to us from a book by Jack London. We fell asleep dreaming of wolf dogs. We all loved to be read to. Our older sisters sometimes read to us, and sometimes I read to the younger children. But just because I could read didn't mean I would pass up listening to someone else read. When father was home, sometimes he would tell us stories, mostly stories of Indian legend and some of his life growing up on the Wind River Reservation in Wyoming. We listened with greedy ears to all his stories. Many of his stories were passed down from previous generations by the elders. As we were far away from Wyoming, we never had the privilege of sitting in the story circles. Father told us from his sittings as a child. Later,

The Story of Two Alaskan Children Growing Up Wild

most of us learned true customs and manners from the elders of the Chickaloon village. Of course there were some kids that took no direction, nor did they learn by their own mistakes, or from the mistakes of others. But that is true of all people.

Some stories are just for entertainment, and others had a lesson in them. I enjoyed both. Always looking for the lesson. But as we were told many times the same lesson stories, most of us learned. We would someday repeat these same stories to our children and our children's children. That is how it has always been done. The dreaming was stopped by the hum of mosquitos. Even though our sleeping bags were pulled tightly over our heads some would get in. The humming and the itching is what would wake you, scratching until bloody scratches adorned both faces and arms.

Getting into the house was no problem for the mosquitoes with gaping cracks in the walls and around the doors. The floor was made of rough-cut boards from a local sawmill. Having not been cured properly before being set for a floor, they dried with wide cracks between them. Not only could hoards of mosquitoes come up through the cracks, most of our silverware and anything else that was small enough ended up under the house. Of course we would go under every now and again to retrieve everything, mostly when we had run out of eating utensils. Even plates turned up under there. We would lie on the floor and play with the puppies through the cracks, dragging something on a string. The puppies pulled on one end, and us on the other. The cracks were no problem except during the summer with the mosquitoes and in the winter when it was cold. A lot of wind came in through those cracks. But we always stuffed socks and other things in the cracks in the winter. Other than that, we didn't mind. As I couldn't sleep with the mosquitoes bothering me so much, I decided to go outside, as maybe a slight breeze would keep most of them off.

I walked over to the pasture and talked to the horses. I noticed that there was what looked like a spotted horse stomping around in the field. On closer inspection it turned out to be Old Polly. There were so many mosquitoes on her and her filly's white coat that they made big black spots on their sides. As I felt sorry for them, I returned to the house and got a bowl of vinegar. I wiped it over her and her filly. Soon she settled down and went to sleep. Her filly lay down also as she could now rest. I used the rest of the bowl of vinegar on the other horses ears and noses. That is where the mosquitoes seemed to be the worst.

The Story of Two Alaskan Children Growing Up Wild

Father had told us there had been cases where some babies had died from the mosquitoes. I could believe it. They are always the worst in spring and fall. The dogs didn't have the trouble so much as the other livestock. They had thick dirty coats and covered their heads and paws with their tails. Sometimes though even they had bloody ears from those ravenous mosquitoes. Father put some kind of grease on their ears if the bites got to bad.

Mother never begrudged the horses the use of some of her vinegar. She felt bad for them as well, and Polly was her favorite anyway. Not being able to get away from the mosquitoes, I went back to bed and held the top of the sleeping bag shut. My choice was overheating and wet with sweat, or be eaten alive. I could live with being too hot. I knew so could all the other kids.

In the morning when the sun came out or a breeze came, the mosquitoes would go away for a while. Even rain would help, and it was past time for rain. There were three or four inches of dust on the roads, which was fun to play in and run horses through. But it meant we had to haul buckets of water to mother's garden.

Mother had all the plants in moats. So, we just had to fill the moats. Which was a large job for four little kids. Mother had made small buckets for the two little girls out of peach cans. She just punched holes near the top and added a wire. Johnny and I had one gallon lard pails. I guess it kept us busy and out from under foot. Although Johnny and I really didn't spend that much time around home if we could help it.

We had a friend that lived four miles away. We would go there and play with him. Some times we would walk another mile past his house to a place were we played in a large sand bank beside a creek. Our friend had a lot of matchbox cars that we made roads for. Holes were dug for houses and garages. It was a lot of fun for the three of us. We would play there for hours. I was happy when morning came. Everyone was. Mother made us pancakes. Our stove was an old army, wood cook stove that father had traded some furs for. It was quite large and had a cook surface on top that was used for frying and grilling. That worked out well for pancakes and things like that as mother could cook a lot of pancakes at once. And as you know, children don't like to wait for their food. We could all eat at the same time, which saved a lot of time and fighting. And of course it had that reservoir, so water was heating for dishes and faces.

After breakfast I never got away fast enough, and my older sister caught me and held me down to comb my hair. It had been neglected for several days and was matted to

The Story of Two Alaskan Children Growing Up Wild

my head in spots. Those spots were a lot thinner after she got done combing out big hunks of it. I screamed and fought, but she just sat on me and continued to comb. She then braided what was left. Telling me if I would comb it more often, it wouldn't hurt so much. I didn't care. I was really mad at her. I didn't see the reason for all that combing and braiding. She really hadn't pulled out that much hair; it just seemed like it. But I knew my little sisters were next, and they would be screaming louder than me. The next to the youngest had very fine hair, and she would roll her head back and forth and hum while she slept. Her hair was always matted tight to her head. It was also very short on the back of her head from combing. Mother put grease in her hair sometimes, so it wouldn't mat so badly. That made a dirty mess though. Well, you don't get lice when you have grease in your hair. So that was a good thing as well.

    I made my escape as soon as my sister stood up. On most days I eluded her so my hair didn't get combed that much. Although I am sure it needed combing. I hardly even picked the sticks out of my braids after climbing trees, unless they were sticking my scalp. It just wasn't important.

    It was my head after all, and I couldn't understand why everyone was so worried about it. I wanted to get as far away from the house as possible today. I was not in a

Johnny & Me

happy mood. Of course as soon as I was out of sight of the house, my mood improved dramatically. I sneaked around the house through the brush, so as to be unseen until I could locate Johnny. He was busy digging holes in an anthill. I threw a small stone next to him. He looked up then abandoned his shovel when I motioned for him to come. We made a quick exit up the hill and away. We sat under a spruce tree and decided what we would do with this day.

There was an old chicken house built into the side of the hill. It was all that remained after our house had burned, and father built another house a quarter mile away. We thought we could make it into a fort. After going in to see what was there, we were assaulted by flies. Johnny grabbed one that was in his face and was just holding it in his hand. It was wiggling around in his hand, so he opened his hand and saw a big yellow jacket. He screamed and shook it out of his hand. Although we were not stung, we did realize those weren't flies. That ended our fort idea for that place.

We then walked another mile to a small cabin that was partially tumbled down to check it out for a fort. This was even better. We rummaged around in the old building and found a pint of cod liver oil. After prying it open we shared it. It must have been great stuff, as we emptied the bottle. We then found half a jar of petroleum jelly. We ate

The Story of Two Alaskan Children Growing Up Wild

that too. It was probably good we didn't find anything else, but we cleaned up the place and decided this was a great place to play. There was a bunk of sorts and a little stove that was still in working order. It had a chimney and a door as well. The sides weren't rusted out to bad. We built a fire and heated some water in a can that we found. We didn't have anything to put in the water, so we just poured it in two smaller cans and pretended to be drinking coffee.

After spending most of the day playing in our new fort we headed home. We both had a bellyache. Mother fed us both a large spoonful of castor oil. Before long we were both in the outhouse where we stayed for most of the evening. Neither Johnny nor I felt much like eating any dinner. In fact, the next morning breakfast wasn't looking that good. Johnny and I moped around for another day before we felt like doing more exploring.

Johnny in car with Mother up front, Hilda on tricycle (behind them) Other sisters in back row on various bikes

CHAPTER 2

The rain finally came. We needed it, but maybe not quite as much as we got. The rivers were over full and

The Story of Two Alaskan Children Growing Up Wild

carrying huge tree root balls. You could hear the big rocks tumbling together in the rivers. The creeks were swollen, but where there were beaver, they never overflowed with much water. The beavers were working around the clock reinforcing their dams. Other creeks weren't so lucky. Our road was washed out. The only way out now was to walk or ride horse back. Our small creek that ran through the pastures was now river size and making deep cut banks through the once level grasses. All the horses and cows had to be moved to higher ground at the base of Castle Mountain. Part of the creek broke from its banks and made a lake where our neighbor's homestead had been. Yet, it still rained. The bodies of moose calves and other small animal that hadn't gotten away from the flooding were seen being washed down the now swollen creeks and rivers.

It was hard to find enough dry wood to cook with. All the children stayed huddled in sleeping bags. There was no need to go out for water, as pots were kept full under the leaks in the roof. The smell of wet sled dogs was almost thick enough to taste, but we didn't mind as some of the dogs lie against us for warmth. Mother pretty much gave up on cooking anything the first day. She gave us each a carrot and a potato. We just ate them raw and that filled our stomachs. It would do until dry firewood was found. The

Johnny & Me

next day our oldest sister brought some wood in from the pile and an ax. After splitting all the outer wood off, the inside was dry. Mother had her do the same with several more chunks. When the fire was going, more wood was brought in to dry beside the stove. The rain had come without anyone covering the woodpile, but now we were warm, and mother could cook again. Although all our meat hanging in the meat house had spoiled from the dampness, we still had some salted-down meat and jerky. The spoiled meat was fed to the sled dogs. What milk the goat gave was made into curdled cheese. That goat didn't give much milk in this weather. Even the chickens gave few eggs. The garden was growing tall and didn't need to be watered. Well at least the lettuce and peas were growing strong among the weeds. The weeds were doing the best. Sadly, not all weeds are good to eat, although we did eat our share of various weeds: dandelion greens, lambs quarters, and even fireweed when it was only an inch or so high.

The rain just kept coming. One soggy day ran into another. Father was out at a camp somewhere. It was unlikely he would be home any time soon as the rivers were too high to cross. Our stores of food were getting kind of low. Johnny and I had been cooped up to long and decided to try fishing in the lake. We wouldn't get much wetter going

The Story of Two Alaskan Children Growing Up Wild

outside. The whole inside of the house was pretty soggy now. At least it would smell better outside in the rain. The older girls had ridden their horses down to a friend's house and had not returned for two days. I guess it was dryer there. They probably had more to eat there also. After walking to the upper lake, we went to a cabin that was on the opposite side. The people that owned it lived in town. They happened to be there, but the weather was too much for them, and they were headed back to town. I don't know why, but they gave us all the food they had left over from their visit. Mostly perishable stuff: a couple oranges and an apple as well as a little meat of some sort.

Well, we forgot about fishing and went home to take mother the food we had been given. We carried the food in two burlap bags. We were little kids, and although I am sure there wasn't that much, it was still heavy work for us slogging through the muddy trail for over a mile. Mother was thankful for the food. She made us kneel down and give thanks. My knees were sore by the time she finally said amen. Boney little knees and hard board floors don't mix that well, but I knew better than to complain. She would have made me wait even longer to get up, as she would then pray for the Lord to forgive my ignorance and take her time about it, I might add. I would have been lucky if that didn't follow with her hand upside my head. So, I just waited her out, and soon enough, she ran out of things to thank God for. I was thanking God myself that she hadn't thought up more stuff to pray about. Not that I thought praying was bad, just that when you are eight years old, you may be thinking of other stuff you would like to be doing other than kneeling on hard boards and waiting for mother to finish talking to God.

    Well, I was thankful for the rain, as we didn't have to carry water for a time. We didn't carry water for quite a while as it turned out. Mother couldn't wash clothes, because they could not be dried. We wore dirty clothes during that rainy time, which was fine with me. I figured they got clean enough walking through the rain. Mother didn't agree, but nothing could be done about it. Even in pouring rain dogs, chickens, and goats need feeding. Of course the milking doe needed to be brought on the porch so mother could milk her out of the rain. Not so much that mother needed to be dry, although that was also a benefit. But the milk would get dirty water in it from off the doe's sides if left in the rain. Mother would wipe her down and wash her udder every day, and with the rain she had to dry her off also. We needed the milk, and I really liked the goats. The kid at her side was mine as mother had given her to me. I was the

The Story of Two Alaskan Children Growing Up Wild

only other person in our family that had such a fondness for goats. She was a doe, and we always kept them. Any buck kids would be weathered and used for meat. When that little doe came fresh the next summer, I would milk her. I was very happy thinking about that. Mother let me milk the old doe sometimes. It was a pleasant job as the old doe had a milking stand that she would jump upon. While she ate her little pan of grain, she would stand still to be milked. But if you took to long, she would get restless and start moving about, sometimes kicking over the milk pail.

 I could milk almost as fast as mother. Some of my sisters weren't as fast and had spilled milk. Mother didn't have any of them milk too often, which is how they liked it I'm sure. The goat was happy to be out of the rain while she was being milked. She didn't want to go back across the yard through the rain to get to her shed. I tried to lead her, but she just planted both front feet and would not move. I pulled as hard as I could, but she out weighed me by quite a bit and paid all my tugging no mind. Finally mother came out, and the goat trotted right over to her shed. She didn't mess with mother. I fed her some hay that was under tarp and locked her and her baby in. They had to be locked in or they might be dinner for some passing hungry predator. It was nice and dry in her shed. In fact, I asked mother if

Johnny & Me

Johnny and I could sleep in there since it was dryer than the house. Mother agreed, and we took our sleeping bags wrapped in a tarp and went out to make a nice hay bed for ourselves.

The goat house was a dry haven for us. Our friend, Mike, from down the road even came to spend the night in the goat house with us a couple of times. He brought an old guitar that was missing a couple of strings. The missing strings really didn't matter as none of us could play anyway. We sang songs and strummed that old guitar all night. The guitar wasn't in tune and neither were we. Not one song was really known by anyone. We all knew a verse here and there. At least we knew the words; we made up our own tunes. The goats didn't seem to mind. In fact, they seemed happy and lay down and slept right through the racket we were making. Although I don't know how they could sleep, as my voice had not improved much since my singing debut as a 4 year old.

As I remember that episode, I may have been the only one having a good time. It was a Christmas service and I had to learn a song. Father taught me a different little song. He didn't expect I would sing that one at the service. Well, when it was my turn to sing, I sang at the top of my lungs. It was bad enough that my voice more closely would

The Story of Two Alaskan Children Growing Up Wild

have matched a cow moose giving birth while being eaten by a pack of wolves. But instead of *"Santa Clause is Coming to Town,"* I sang something about Santa riding his sleigh in his BVDs with his hind end swinging in the breeze. Father was trying to shush me, but I just sang louder. That kind of finished that Christmas service. The pastor gave father some pretty hard looks. He knew where I had gotten that song.

    We slept in the goat house for over a month waiting for the rain to stop. The goats were glad to see us go, I am sure, as we slept in their hay feeder, and they had to eat on the floor. After all, they were goats, and it was okay for them to eat off the floor. I think we took a couple extra days to move back into the house when the rain stopped. It took that long for the house to dry out. It took another week after that for father to be able to cross the rivers. And even then, it was too dangerous to cross with a pack string. So, he left all the horses except his large draft-cross gelding which he was sure had the best chance of crossing safely. It was another two weeks before father went back for the rest of the horses. It took a while to get the horses home as a lot of the trails had been washed out. New trails had to be cut around the washed out areas. Some places had to be dug out and filled with rocks. A lot of trees had fallen and had to

Johnny & Me

be cut out of the trails by hand with a bow saw and axe. It had rained for two full months, and not just a drizzle. There were now lakes where there had been low valleys. Our road had to be rebuilt. A new road was cut into the hillside as the old road was now under water. It dried out somewhat, but due to the creek changing channels; it was never dry enough for a road again. Father had to pull cars and trucks out of the mud holes in the road with a team of horses. The road was not passable for quite some time, even after being repaired with a lot of CAT work. Our friend Mike's father had a CAT, a large excavator. Since he owed father money, he did all the road repair.

The neighbor's fields were now a lake complete with fish as the creek now ran that way. There were some ponds that were left with no creek and started to dry up. They were full of land locked salmon. Father had us all work to drag a net across the pond and harvest all the large fish for smoking, and a few mother fried for dinner. All the small fish we could catch were hauled to the big lake and released. I think we must have released several thousands baby fish. We hauled them to the lake in every bucket and can we could find by horse-drawn wagon. I don't think too many fish were missed as father had us drag the ponds several times to make sure. Father said by saving the fish we were

The Story of Two Alaskan Children Growing Up Wild

not only helping the fish, we were helping ourselves since later they would be in the lake to fish out in the future.

Our neighbor could no longer farm his fields and moved away. I think his wife didn't like the country anyway. His farm was later subdivided and sold in five-acre lots, but that was a few years later after the creek had been moved to run a meandering path to another lake. When the land was divided into five-acre lots, it was all creek side property. The oats in the field were over six feet tall. There would be plenty of feed for the livestock this winter. Maybe we wouldn't have to go live in the small shack on the tide flats this winter. Maybe we could go to school. That was a happy thought. I loved school. Some of my older sisters only went to sixth grade. They never had a chance to go to school much, and when they turned sixteen, they could quit and get married. I wanted to go to school, and I was sure I never wanted to get married. It seemed like a lot of work to me. Of course, what eight-year-old would think anything else?

The tall oats made a great hiding place for Johnny and I. Father never thought much of our building forts in his winter-feed, but we didn't ruin much. We spent time in our fort, making spears and arrows from the dried wild celery stalks. The stalks were hollow; so we filled them with dirt and sealed the ends with small sticks. Which made a place

Johnny & Me

to add a sharpened nail. They were really quite deadly on squirrels, birds, and rabbits, but only lasted for one use. We made a lot of them. Mother was happy with any meat we brought for her to cook. We ate a lot of small game and even a few fish were speared from the creek. The fish would usually get away as they came off the nails or our spears broke. Some times we could catch them any way, as they were wounded. Mostly, we could trap the fish or catch them with our hands if they were big enough.

The lake had much bigger fish, but it was a mile away to where we fished on our pontoon boat. The creek was only fifty yards away from the house. We fished in the creek mostly when mother ordered us to stay close to home. Mother had to catch us early in the morning though, as we always tried to get away before anyone was up. Most of the time, we did get away, but not today. When we slipped out the back way, mother was waiting by the clothesline. She had a full days' chores lined up for us. After all that rain there was a lot of things that needed fixing. The spring box in the creek had washed full of dirt and debris and needed cleaning out. That was where we started. It wasn't a bad job. We got to play in the creek as we shoveled out the box. We drug that job out as long as we could, that is until mother came out to check on our progress. From there we

The Story of Two Alaskan Children Growing Up Wild

moved to cleaning the chicken house and changing the grass in the nest boxes. Now, that was down right disgusting. We didn't waste time in there. We wanted to get out of that chicken house as soon as possible. Mother soon arrived there, bringing new grass for the nests and telling us to scrape the floor a little better. We set to work with a little more energy, as mother said after we finished that job she had made us some sandwiches that were waiting on the table. We just ran to the creek to clean up; we were pretty dirty by that time. Lunch was even better than promised. There was a cup of milk for each of us. Now that the rain had stopped, the goat was giving more milk. Of course, it helped that mother had weaned the kid from her side. We now got all the milk. Mother could even make bread pudding.

On one of the days father was home, a preacher came to visit. Father got a couple of chairs, and they sat on the porch drinking coffee. Johnny was standing next to the preacher, whom everyone called Uncle Hubard. Uncle Hubard kept leaning back in the chair and raising the front legs off the porch. On one of the down strokes the chair landed on Johnny's foot. Johnny kept trying to get Uncle Hubard's attention by tapping him on the shoulder and repeating "Uncle Hubard, please move your chair. Uncle

Johnny & Me

Hubard, please move your chair." to no avail. After a bit, Johnny leaned very close to the preacher's ear and yelled, "DOD DAMN IT UNCLE HUBARD, DIT OFF MY FOOT!!"
That got everyone's attention. Well, he did get off his foot. Father's face was a little red, but he was also trying hard not to smile. I think that kind of ended that cheery little visit.

Mother reminded us that we needed to get a move on to repair as much as possible because winter was coming. We would also be starting school again in two weeks. Summer had been washed away with the rain. We had only hunting season left to look forward to. We wouldn't go back to school until all our caribou and moose tags were full. That would be the end of our freedom for a while. Father had already left with the big girls for the hunting camps. They were actually the ones that hunted; we were just along to claim the kills. Not that we had much trouble with fish and game people being up in the mountains where we hunted. They mostly left native people alone. We had to have those tags filled to have enough food for the winter. Father trapped during the winter and wouldn't be there to provide for us very often. It was up to mother to make our supplies last as long as possible. If we ran short of food, there was not much chance we would get more. Sometimes we would have to eat a horse if nothing else

The Story of Two Alaskan Children Growing Up Wild

could be found. That hadn't happened often, but it had happened enough that mother was careful to ration our winter stores. Of course we would eat the chickens and goats before we touched a horse.

Mother had us fill the cracks in the walls of the cabin with moss mixed with mud. The wind blew a lot in the winter. The muddy moss dried hard as cement and would keep the wind out during the long cold winter. Wool socks that came from the army base were split and chinked into the cracks from the inside to keep the dirt out. It was a job little fingers did well. We also piled dirt around the bottom of the cabin, leaving only a small hole that was covered with a board. A child could still crawl under to retrieve anything lost through the floor cracks.

It seemed mother never ran out of things for us to do. Since the four smallest children were home, we had to fill in for the big girls as well as do our chores. There were lots of extra things that needed to be done to prepare for winter. Going back to school was looking better each day.

Mother even sent us out to check all the trees near the house for halters and ropes. Then sent us off to the pastures for the same reason. It seems that children have a habit of leaving ropes and other tack wherever they happened to have been last. We even found a saddle on a

Johnny & Me

log near the field. I guess that was where someone had unsaddled and turned their horse loose. It would be to late to find anything after it snowed, and snow was coming soon.

While Johnny and I searched the field for forgotten tack, we were startled and frightened to hear a most horrible roaring and thrashing in the trees near the field. Of course we had to find out what was causing such a disturbance. We thought maybe it was a dragon or some such creature. Creeping into the woods and trying to seem as small as possible, we soon were near enough to see the cause of all the uproar. It was a very large bull moose destroying a small stand of cottonwood saplings. He was tearing them off at ground level. He never noticed us as we faded back into the trees.

Forgotten was the chore mother had sent us to do. Instead, we decided to get someone with a gun to shoot this moose because it was very important for winter meat. Since no one was home but mother, we decided to go for the neighbor. It was only one half mile, and we ran as fast as we could. Johnny, being the faster by far, was there ahead of me and was on his way back with our neighbor gun in hand before I got there. It was no trouble getting into range for a good shot as that bull was having way to much fun

The Story of Two Alaskan Children Growing Up Wild

destroying those trees. Our hired gun was able to get close enough to take the bull down with a single shot.

Johnny ran for home to get mother. When he returned with mother and the babies in tow. We all helped her butcher. Even the neighbor helped, as it was a very big moose and a very large job for a small woman and four little children. Mother shared part of the meat with our neighbor. But he wouldn't take much because he knew mother had a lot of children to feed and was mostly by herself. That night we had a wonderful boiled moose heart.

Mother gave Johnny and I most of the fat from the top of the heart to show her pride in us. We were the little heroes, at least mother made us feel that way. Long forgotten was finishing our chores. With full bellies, we slept late into the morning, only waking when mother shook us out of our dreams. She said, "You must get up children. There is much to do today. I think it is going to snow in the next day or so."

After breakfast we finished looking for the tack scattered about the place. The rest of the vegetables were put in the hill and covered for winter. All the tools were hung in the shed, at least all we could find. Mother was busy canning meat that day and several days after that. There was no refrigeration except the weather, and that needed to cool a bit as flies still came out in mid-day. Although we did keep the meat in a screened in shed, it kept out most of the flies and let the air circulate, keeping the meat fairly cold and aging.

We ate meat for all our meals for a while. All the organ meat didn't get canned and would spoil sooner than the rest of the meat. Very little meat was lost, and that was just scraps we fed the puppies. Mother always told us that everything was used but the squeals. We even would break the large bones and extract the marrow. It was used to make marrow soup, or just removed after roasting and eaten. It is high in energy and tastes good as well. Actually, we children had a tendency to fight over it. After all, it was a real treat. All of us loved fat. We always tried to get as much as possible. Father always would fry himself a large piece of fat whenever he got a fat moose or caribou. Fat also helps when cooking stick meat. Sometimes, I would just eat the fat raw. We all ate raw moose meat when it was frozen. You just shave off thin slices and add salt. I guess that even city people eat raw meat; only they call it "steak tartare."

Mother had a meat grinder that was run on kid power. We ground quite a lot of the poorer parts to make smoked sausage. Smoked sausage doesn't need to be frozen or canned. You just hang it in the shed. Of course it

The Story of Two Alaskan Children Growing Up Wild

is not very safe from children there. We really didn't eat too much of the sausage as mother needed it for winter food. Well, actually mother reinforced that fact with a willow switch. Jerky was also made. We did tend to eat more of that, but a lot of jerky was made so we could afford to eat more. We even saved the bladder to blow up and kick around for a ball. The bull's horns were added to father's horn and skull pile.

Father's horn pile now would fill a large truck, and eventually did as the horns were sold to carvers and taxidermists. So even the horns and skulls helped provide food and supplies. Nothing was wasted. Mother was right; it did snow a couple days later. Which did not stop Johnny and I from going into the woods. We went bird hunting around the lake. We didn't get any birds, but ran into Old Minnie coming home. She had been gone for a couple of months. But here she was with a red bald-faced colt in tow. Johnny and I just climbed on and let her take us home.

We met father and the big girls coming home through the field. Father asked us where we had found Old Minnie. Well we told him we had found her in a meadow way up in the hills, which was a rather big lie. But we got a lot of praise out of it for being real dandy horse hunters. I don't think we ever did tell anyone anything different. Although

Johnny & Me

father probably knew that Old Minnie had just coming back home because of the snow. Father was rarely fooled by our stories. Mother was actually a little easier to fool, but she let us think we got away with things more often than she believed. Once again we were feeling mighty proud of ourselves.

Father and the big girls had brought a whole pack train loaded with meat. It was now cold enough to keep the meat through the winter. A good amount of the meat was salted away in wooden barrels. That would be used when all the frozen meat was gone. The salted meat would turn dark and tasted good just sliced off and eaten raw. No one ever got sick from it; so I guess it was cured. I know I ate my share, but it took a month or so to cure. You could always slice it up, as it never froze. I would just open a barrel and slice off what I wanted to eat whenever I wanted. As plenty was made, it never mattered how much we ate. We always ate a lot when food was plentiful as we went hungry when it was not. I think it was the same for most bush folks.

It was nice just sitting behind the woodstove and listening to father and the older girls talk of their hunting trip. Between the wall and the stove was the warmest place in the house. The four little kids could all fit there on the floor. With being full from supper and the warmth of the stove, we soon were asleep. Someone hauled us off to bed, as that is where I woke that next morning.

The next few days were used up just storing the meat, but not for the younger kids. We spent most of our time sledding on the new snow. We each harnessed a dog to pull us. It was great fun for the dogs and us. Later, it would be just work for all of us. When the meat was safely stored father rounded everyone up to haul all of the oat shocks that had been drying in the fields back to the feed yard. I think Johnny and I spent more time catching mice that had homes under the shocks. Father never got angry with us since all the oat hay was stored in a few days, and we were assured we would stay there in the valley that winter.

A hog butchering plant in Eagle River brought a load of crackling cakes that father always traded for in the fall. They are cakes of hog fat and skin after the lard is rendered and pressed out. Each weighed about fifty pounds. We used them to mix in the dog food that was cooked every week. They were stacked by the big fire pit in the dog lot. All the children would pry off the hard pork rind pieces to eat. The cakes would stay good as long as it didn't get too warm that they turned rancid. I ate them rancid well many

Johnny & Me

times when I was hungry. It didn't make much difference to me.

All four little kids were taken to the mountains to retrieve the rest of the meat. That was to cover our game tags. It was a cold but short trip. It was not at all fun. We would be happy to return to school everyday. At least the school was warm. Father collected all his winter supplies and loaded his big sled for his winter trapping. He would leave soon, and we would not see him again for several months. He usually would come back for a short stay around Christmas, but not always. If the trapping was good, sometimes he would stay and continue trapping.

Father usually took nine or eleven dogs. His sled was big and heavy with supplies when he left and with furs and also rocks and horns that had been collected in the summer on the return trip. Johnny's birthday arrived on October twenty-fifth with not much fan fair. We were again the same age, well until January when I would turn nine. Mother baked a cake and frosted it with sugar glaze. Everyone had made something for him. I gave him my favorite big marble. Johnny had wanted that marble for quite sometime. He had tried to win it from me on many occasions. Johnny was quite a good marble player. He had won most of the good marbles from the neighbor children at school. There must

The Story of Two Alaskan Children Growing Up Wild

have been a couple hundred marbles in his marble pouch.

We never had chain saws in those days. Only a buck saw or bow saw as some called them. Woodcutting was a lot of work. Most wood was cut into logs then hauled by dog sled and cut into stove size at home. Everyone took their turn sawing. Although only the bigger girls fell the trees we all brought them home. A lot of our time was used getting wood. With wood and other chores there was little time for play in the winter. The days were short anyway. We went to school and returned home in the dark. We rode horses or used a dog team to get to school. If we rode horse, we had to tie a bundle of oat hay behind the saddle to feed them. The horses were tied to a tree in an area across the path from the school. If we brought dogs, they were tied beside the creek so they could drink. Either way, it kept us from having to walk the five miles to the school.

Some days when the wind was blowing and it was to far below zero, we never went to school. The stove held us close on those days. Mother would not send the smaller children out to do chores, fearing they would get frostbitten or lost in the blowing snow. That did not make the older girls like us any better, as they had to do our chores as well as theirs. The older girls didn't treat us badly though; they loved us. But they would give us some ugly looks. We could

Johnny & Me

live with that. It was a lot better than out in the freezing weather.

The Story of Two Alaskan Children Growing Up Wild

Me and my sisters in winter

CHAPTER 3

The snow was deep by the first of November. The wind piled it into deep drifts and packed it hard. We could walk on most of it, except in the woods or the backsides of some of the drifts. We dug under the drifts and made snow forts. The drifts were piled deep enough that there was room to stand inside our snow caves. Well, we weren't very tall after all, and the drifts might not have been quite as deep compared to an adult. Nevertheless, they made great snow forts, and we could play out of the wind. The wind never seemed to stop blowing in the winter.

We dug all the way to the ground, which seemed to make nice homes for some of the sled dogs too, because they moved right in. I guess they wanted out of the wind as well. We didn't mind sharing. One of the female dogs took up housekeeping in our best fort. It was fine for a while until the puppies got to walking around and leaving land mines of waste all over the place. We had to abandon that fort.

I don't think many of us had real gloves. Sometimes we used old gloves that father had thrown away because of the holes, but most of the time we used wool socks that came from the army base. Those socks worked fine most of the time, although occasionally you had to remove them to tie a rope, unsnap a dog, or some other chore that required thumbs. Socks never hampered the making of snowballs though. We spent a lot of time making snowballs and piling them to waylay our older sisters any chance we had. Our faces got washed with hard snow more than once from our sisters, but that never held us back from our next opportunity at a snowball fight.

The Story of Two Alaskan Children Growing Up Wild

Thinking about it, those older girls never gave us too hard of a time. They had just as much fun as we did; even our chores were made into games like who could chop the most wood or feed the horses the fastest. We never had to feed the cow since it had been sold to a farmer in town in the fall. When the snow was deep and the wind had blown it hard, the horses had a hard time pawing for food. Then we had to supplement with oat hay, which had been stored in stacks. When we had oat hay, we could arrange bundles of oats in stacks to make caves. Mother would let us sleep outside in the haystacks when we didn't have to go to school the next day. It was nice and cozy in the hay, although it didn't take us long to get back to the house in the morning after we got up. Most of the time it was warmer in the hay at night than in the house where the wind blew through the cracks.

The older girls moved back into the house that winter to save on wood. Not as much woodcutting was needed for only one house. All the saddle blankets were hung against the walls to keep out as much wind as possible. A pack tarp was laid on the board floor to cover those cracks as well. That helped keep the house a bit warmer, and the smaller children spent most of our time behind the cook stove anyway because it was the warmest place in the house. Of

Johnny & Me

course we were behind the stove only when we were in the house. We spent a lot of time outdoors, as we still had chores even in the coldest of weather. Animals have to eat and drink too. A lantern was hung in the chicken house each night to keep the chickens from freezing. The older girls had that chore because those old lanterns were not safe and could sometimes catch fire.

Mother only used the gas lanterns for a short time each night since the gas cost a lot, and the chickens needed it more than we did. So we used gas lanterns in the house only for dinner and homework. The rest of the time we used grease lamps. Those are just grease or fat in a bowl with a rag wick. They give enough light to see in the house, but they smoke a lot. Thankfully with all the cracks in the house, we wouldn't suffocate. Although grease lamps are dangerous in that they can fall over or the whole thing sometimes just bursts into flame. You have to put them where they can't start a house fire. On those long winter nights, mother always read to us, mostly from the Bible. We never tired of listening to her read. With the warm fire and dim lights, it never took long for everyone to fall asleep.

Morning came early for everyone, as there were chores before breakfast even on school days. Yes, livestock eat and drink in the morning too. The lantern had to be

The Story of Two Alaskan Children Growing Up Wild

refueled for the day to keep chicken coop above freezing. Any eggs were usually frozen though, but we used them anyway. There were not that many eggs in the winter. Mother was happy with there was. She never complained much about things. She just worked with what we had and was pleased to get anything extra.

Some mornings it was hard to make the trip to the outhouse because moose would lie between it and the house. Sometimes the moose would get up and walk away without too much trouble. That was not the norm though. Usually they would get up on the fight. Moose can stomp you to death with very little effort, and have done so for many people and dogs. Dogs are usually of little help as they bark at the moose making them mad. Then the dogs run to the nearest person for safety. Nobody wants that person to be him. No one can outrun a moose in deep snow. So usually, we would try to detour around the moose or just go to the bathroom behind the nearest snowdrift.

On one such morning as I was trying to make my early morning bathroom trip, my dog, Snooks, ran past me and started barking at a moose in the face. I think she was surprised at the speed of that cow moose. The moose jumped up and trampled Snooks into the snow. It was a good thing that snow was deep. I thought Snooks was dead

Johnny & Me

for sure. I started yelling and throwing icicles as fast as I could, trying to stay out of sight around the corner of the house. The moose grew tired of looking for Snooks under the snow where she had been buried by her hooves and decided to move on and just walked off. That was lucky for Snooks and me as it turned out. After the moose left, I went to dig Snooks out of the snow, expecting the worst. Instead of a little dead body, I found Snooks knocked out but not much worse for the wear. She had a rather deep cut between her ears, but lived just fine after that. Snooks never barked at moose again. I guess she learned something from the experience and seemed a lot more timid after that.

While that experience was not the last of the many moose encounters that occurred through the years, it was one of my most memorable ones. Mother poured turpentine into the cut on Snooks head to clean it and added a few stitches. I had to use another dog for my leader that day. Snooks were good to go in a couple of days and no longer chased moose on the way to school. I was always on time for school after that. I really liked school. There was a small library at school, and I read every book.

Our school was just one classroom for all the grades. Most of the children were from our family. The rest of the children were from the surrounding homestead families.

The Story of Two Alaskan Children Growing Up Wild

They had moved into the area in the few years after father had built a road. It wasn't much of a road, but it worked well for our horses and us. The other homesteaders combined their efforts and had improved the road but only as far as their homesteads. We were the last homestead on the road. Over it was still not a great road, and cars got stuck in the mud in summer and snow in winter. Cars stuck in bad weather ironically worked out for us. Father made a bit of money pulling them out of the mud or snow with his team of horses.

Johnny was a class clown and kept everyone laughing. The teacher never cared much for his jokes and pranks. Once, she decided to punish him for disrupting the class, but of course you have to catch someone in order to punish them. Johnny never mad it that easy. When she went to Johnny's desk, Johnny would run the other way, jumped up on her desk, and after knocking everything onto the floor, he slipped and landed in the garbage can. His head and legs were sticking out, and he had to be pulled free. The whole class was cheering and laughing. The teacher couldn't spank him since everyone was on his side. Finally, the teacher just gave up and went to her trailer, leaving my older sister in charge.

We liked having my sister teach us, as she made

Johnny & Me

learning fun. Our sister never had all the problems that teacher had. We liked her and listened to what she told us. Besides, we had to go home with our sister. Our sister knew as much as the teacher, and therefore never advanced above eighth grade in many subjects. The teacher we had was unable to teach what she herself didn't know. She was not big on math of any sort. I am sure the teacher was fine with elementary grades. At eight years old I knew more about history than she did, but of course I read everything. That was not our best school year, as far as learning was concerned.

Thanksgiving came, and mother baked a large ham from one of our pigs we'd raised. I was hoping she would cook those two geese, but she was saving them for Christmas. We had a lovely dinner anyway. There were potatoes and gravy, peas and carrots, which mother had canned, and of course homemade bread. Mother made the best bread in the world. There was pie for desert. Everyone went to bed stuffed and happy.

Mother prayed for father who was alone on his trapline. We all made our own prayers for father and everyone else. After all, it was a time to be thankful for all our friends, most of which were animals. We all missed having father home with us. Not many Thanksgivings were ever spent

The Story of Two Alaskan Children Growing Up Wild

with father, because it is right in the middle of his best trapping season.

As Christmas approached everybody was busy for weeks making gifts of one sort or another. My oldest sister was busy making new dog harnesses for everyone. The girls that could knit and crochet made scarves, hats, and mittens. Mother had been making quilts all year. I'm not so sure the younger children made any grand gifts. We mostly put beads on strings with bear claws and antler ends for necklaces. Johnny carved a wooden spoon for mother. It was rough, but he was only just eight years old. He did pretty good job on the spoon, and mother kept it for many years. The two smallest girls colored pictures for everyone. We all were excited waiting for the big day.

Johnny and I were happy to see those ornery geese hanging in the meat house. Mother had plucked them clean while we were at school. We had an extra week off before Christmas, as the teacher went to visit her family for the holidays. Her leaving was as good a present as we could get from the school. We had a lot of time to catch up on things that needed to be done at home. There was also time for play. Winter days are so short, and with school we had little time to play outside. We took advantage of the time off of school and went sledding with the dogs on the river,

Johnny & Me

pretending to be Sergeant Preston of the Royal Canadian Police.

Some people from the church in town hiked up our road and brought us some gifts like Jergen's lotion in little bottles shaped like Eskimo dolls. I don't know what happened to the lotion inside, but the bottles were played with for a long time. We never had a lot of toys, so treasured what we had. For Johnny, they brought a baseball and mitt, which were promptly lost in the snow. We found it the next spring none the worse for the winter spent under the snow. They also brought mother a mirror and hairbrush. Maybe they thought she should get a look at herself?

They also brought some canned fruit so mother could make pies and a canned ham, which mother put away for another occasion, since we had a ham from our pigs and she had already killed the two geese. Mother spent the last few days before Christmas making pies and bread and cookies. Mother even made snow ice cream treats. Christmas Eve came and everything was ready for Christmas dinner. The only thing missing was father. We all hoped he would make it home for Christmas.

The older girls cut a nice spruce tree and set it up in the corner. We had made decorations from paper and colored yarn and even some cans were cut in spirals to

The Story of Two Alaskan Children Growing Up Wild

hang in the branches. One of the older girls found an old bird's nest and added it to a branch. It looked great there with some colored paper in it. Mother got out her paper angel, one of the older girls had made in a past year. It was a beautiful Christmas tree. At least that's how I remember it. All our homemade presents were placed under it. We were all quite proud of ourselves. We all went to bed Christmas Eve waiting for father's return. We were very sad children that night. Tomorrow would be not quite as nice without father.

Early the next morning, the dogs started barking and woke us all. It was father. He had made it after all, even if somewhat late. His sled was full of wonderful things. He had went to town and sold his furs on his way home. Father had bought a small puppy for one of the older girls and a pair of Levis for each of us. He also bought a big box of chocolate covered cherries and some oranges for us to share. He brought mother the most beautiful moccasins with fur and beads. It was a very exciting day. Mother and the older girls worked all day to cook a wonderful dinner. Father helped us younger children do all the chores and even had time to take us sledding down the hill. We came home when we were good and cold. The timing was just right, and dinner was almost ready. After washing up and helping to set the

Johnny & Me

table, we all sat down to a prayer followed by a very wonderful meal. Mother had even baked rolls, and there was a large butter topped roll for each of us. We were very rich that Christmas, rich with love and happiness.

The Story of Two Alaskan Children Growing Up Wild

Father at our cabin

CHAPTER 4

Father stayed home for a couple weeks after Christmas. He repaired the sled, which needed some of the rawhide replaced because it had been chewed by the dogs. Harnesses had to be replaced. Father was happy to receive some new harnesses from my older sister for his Christmas gift. One of his dogs had puppies while he was on the trap line. The puppies had ridden in a bag on the sled while the mother pulled. That would be the only time they rode in the sled. They would grow up and later work in the team.

The puppies we raised were usually broke to harness while they still were puppies. The children would hook them to little sleds as soon as they could keep up with the big dogs. It was play for the puppies and us. If the puppies didn't learn to pull when they were hooked as puppies, they usually didn't turn out to be good sled dogs. Those puppies were sold or given away for pets.

Father had a big radio that we got to listen to when he was home. The radio was hooked up to a car battery. That's where we learned about the Lone Ranger, The Shadow, and many other radio show heroes. Sitting around in a circle listening to the radio was real family time. We were also treated to father's stories on many nights. We learned about the monstrous animal that lived in the mountains, just waiting for children and livestock to stray. There was the terrible helliphontis. Father drew pictures of that monster. It kind of looked like a long bear-cat with a long bushy tail, big claws, and big teeth. We were all dually terrorized, and of course everyone told of being sure they had glimpsed it at one time or another. What a bunch of little storytellers we were. Mother and father had a lot of good entertainment with our stories I am sure. It was all in

The Story of Two Alaskan Children Growing Up Wild

good fun and made evenings a time of happiness.

Many a night father would sit at the table writing letters to hunting clients by lamplight. We had to be quiet so he could think. Nobody wanted father to get mad. That was never a pleasant thing. Although father never spanked us much, he would scare us with his voice. Johnny and I would lay behind the stove and whisper. If we got to loud, father would yell at us. That was enough to quiet us down for the rest of the evening.

While he was home, father shot two of the moose that were keeping us out of the yard. They were stored under snow, and their meat would help get us through the winter. They were cows with a couple of inches of fat on their backs. We all ate nice fat steaks for a while. Mother made a brisket roast that first day. We enjoyed chewing on the fat covered bones. Brisket fat is different than steak fat; it tends to be chewy. We loved it.

Father made rawhide strings from some of the hide. It doesn't make the best strings because it tends to break more than beef hide, but it works for repair on the trail when nothing else is available. The sleds always needed repair. Any time a dog was loose, they would chew on the rawhide bindings. It is wise to have spare strips of rawhide along on any trip.

Johnny & Me

To soon it was time for father to return to the trap line and for us to return to school days. No longer were horses used to make the trip to school. We would get too cold riding horses. Also the horses needed all their energy to keep warm and make it through the winter alive. Instead, we used regular dog sleds now, as it was too cold to lie on a hand sled. The dog sleds kept you warm, as you had to work the sled with your weight and also run behind. The little children rode in the sled in a sleeping bag.

We had two sleds: one with three children and one with four children. Two of the older girls would share the runners, taking turns running. It also made for a much faster trip, as the girls raced each other. Sometimes, a dogfight would ensue in the passing. That happened more than once because the dogs don't like to be passed and would lunge into the passing team. Dogfights are hard to break up and can result in severe injuries to one or more dogs, as well as the person or persons trying to separate them. There were a few times through the years that a dog would get killed if the fight was not broken up fast enough. Rarely did we get bitten though, as everyone would help pulling the sleds apart so the dogs couldn't reach each other. A bullwhip was used to discourage further fighting. The harnesses were usually tangled and had to be straightened out. This

The Story of Two Alaskan Children Growing Up Wild

sometimes took a long time and caused us to be late to school, but it couldn't be helped. Well, it could have if the racing stopped I suppose, but we could see no good reason to do that. The dogfights continued through the winter.

In mid-January we had a Chinook wind that melted most of the snow. We were still able to sled to school. The road became icy, and our sleds could still slide on ice. There were a few places were it thawed all the way to the dirt, but they were few and far between. If you hit one of those patches of dirt, you would come to an abrupt stop. Sometimes, it would catapult the person on the runners forward into the sled or onto the road. The handler bars hitting you in the stomach was not that great either. The road was slick though and had water running over the ice. It was hard to stand up without holding on to something. The sled was also hard to stop, even with the brake. Chains had to be wrapped around the runners to get down the hill without running over the dogs. We had to turn a hard left-hand turn at the very bottom of the hill to reach the school. If you missed the turn, you would fall over a high rock bank where the Chickaloon River snaked across the valley at the bottom of the hill. Open places were abundant in the ice of the river. No one wanted to wind up in the river. If you fell in, you would be pulled under the ice on a short trip to the

Johnny & Me

Matanuska River. This would be followed by a longer trip on to the Cook Inlet. Getting out of either river would not be an option. You'd be dead for sure.

I liked to get out of the sled and make my own way down that hill on foot. I was afraid of winding up in the river. My oldest sister had tried to ski down that hill and found herself bridging such a place in the ice. She had to be rescued by the other children. Another sister roped her, and we all pulled her back. None of us ever tried skiing down that hill again. Sometimes we learned from our mistakes, but not all the time. That January thaw spoiled all the meat we had under the snow for us, but it didn't go to waste, as we fed it to the dogs. We were short on food the rest of the winter. Thankfully, we had mother's vegetables stored in the hillside. Toward spring we had no food at all except some flour and beans. We had to eat both of the goats and most of the chickens to survive. It was good we had them, or we would have had to eat a horse or some of the dogs. We needed them for transportation, and they were how father made a living so it would have been a last resort. A few of the puppies would have been okay as we had a few more than we needed, and they weren't working yet. But it never quite came to that thankfully, at least that winter anyway.

The weather stayed warm for two weeks then

The Story of Two Alaskan Children Growing Up Wild

returned cold with a vengeance. The horses could no longer go out to dig for grass as it was frozen under a couple inches of ice and were entirely dependent on our haystack. As this was not originally planned, the hay was rationed. The horses became thin and very hungry. One of the racehorses that had come from the track was near death, and mother had one of the big girls shoot him. That horse couldn't take the cold and short rations quite as well as the mustangs we had. We fed him to the dogs as well. The dogs had a better living than we did and weren't as hungry either.

    My birthday came at the end of January, and nobody even noticed except my brother Johnny. He had carved me a wooden knife. I was surprised and pleased. The day to day keeping us fed was all mother thought of during those times. I guess it was poor planning for me to have been born in the heart of winter. Soon February came, and the days grew longer. The sun came back for a little longer each day. That is on the days it wasn't snowing. The winds were strong and continued through most of the month, but they were no longer warm.

    At the end of the month, the sun started to warm the trees and bring up the sap. Now we could start tapping the birch trees to make syrup and sugar. Johnny and I did most of the tapping. Everyone was excited to eat the first batch. Not having much for so long, the birch sugar was good. It takes a lot of sap to make one small pan of sugar. Mother cut it into squares, saving only a very small piece for herself. We ate it like candy. Johnny and I took ours and sat behind the stove. We held the sugar in our cheeks like squirrels, to savor it as long as possible. It wasn't to fill our bellies, but to fill our spirits with hope for an early spring and an abundance of growing things. The lean days would soon be over. The rivers and lakes were beginning to thaw. Fish would soon be available.

Mother made us pancakes, and now we had syrup. How wonderful that was, even with out butter! Beaver season was here, and beaver tail in beans was another gift. Things were looking up. It wouldn't be long till trapping was over, and father was home again. Well, at least for a short while. He would be gone again on spring bear hunts during April and May. Black bear season was always open. Father could take hunters out for black bear at any time the bears were not hibernating. Bears don't really sleep through the winter. They get up every now and again to walk around, even in the middle of winter. If you find a bear den in winter, it's an easy way to get meat. It can be dangerous though if extreme caution is not used. When you wake up a bear, it is

The Story of Two Alaskan Children Growing Up Wild

not very happy and can turn the hunter into its dinner instead.

Our oldest sister had a birthday the first of March. Her birthday actually fell on February 29th, but mother had moved it up to the first of March so she could have a birthday each year. I don't think she did as good as I did for gifts. Johnny never carved her anything special for her birthday. It was just another day closer to spring, but that was good also.

The days were growing longer. The trip home from school was no longer in the dark. The roads were melted to the dirt, and the sleds were no longer used. It was back to riding horses. Some of the horses were in poor condition and couldn't be ridden. We doubled up on the stronger ones. The horses were now turned loose on the hillsides next to the school during the day where they could dig out new shoots of grass. They never ran away, as they were hungry for the new green of spring. They just spent the day pawing for roots and shoots.

As the days grew longer and warmed the hillsides, Johnny and I tended to spend more time sitting on the mosses and pine needles on the hill over looking the school than attending the school. I don't think anyone cared. The teacher was tired of us, and who was she going to tell

Johnny & Me

anyway? When it got closer to spring, we quit going all together. We figured we'd learned enough for that year any way. The older girls had to help father now, and the little girls had no one to take them to school. I can't say the teacher was unhappy seeing us go. She probably did a victory dance around the classroom. Well maybe not, but I'm sure she was pleased anyway.

The sun had begun to melt the ice on the edges of the lakes. The fish were hungry for sunlight and you could watch them swimming just under the edge of the ice. The fish were preparing to spawn in the creeks that run into the lakes. Johnny and I didn't need any encouragement to get out our fishing poles. Actually most of our fishing poles were just a willow stick with fishing line tied at the end. We didn't need more than that to catch fish. Sometimes, we could use our hands to catch the fish as they were running up the small creeks to spawn. They don't bite when they are spawning. They are also not paying much attention to their surroundings and are reasonably easy to catch with your bare hands. The first day we went fishing, we came home with a dozen nice big trout for mother to cook. We even saved the eggs to fry up. The dogs got the fish heads and cleanings. I don't remember trout tasting that good ever before. I even ate the fins that were fried up nice and crispy.

The Story of Two Alaskan Children Growing Up Wild

We fished most every day for a while. That was all the meat we had until father brought a bear home. It was a skinny bear with not much fat on it, but it tasted wonderful. Father had good trapping during the beaver season. He traded his furs and made the trip to Anchorage to replenish our food stores. The good times were back again. We had plenty to eat now. We never thought farther than the present moment, as we were children. When we had food, we never thought much about the times when there would be none.

All of us children seemed to be a headache for father. He seemed to think we were not growing up civilized enough. Father sent to Wyoming for his widowed sister to come and teach us to be more civilized. I can't speak for the older girls, but I was not interested in being a lady; not one little bit. I made up my mind to be as mean as I could. Maybe our auntie would not bother with me? After all, there were plenty of other older girls to teach how to be a lady. Maybe she would go back to Wyoming and not notice me if I stayed out of sight. Well, those were just daydreams. I became her number one target. I guess I was the most in need of manners of the bunch of us. It just made me more determined than ever to be myself. All she ever got from me was a hard time. After a while, she mostly gave up, and that suited me fine. She was always kind, and I didn't know how to deal well with her.

She really was a nice lady. There was no reason for me to be so ornery. All the other girls learned to knit, tat, and other things like cooking. I missed out and was sorry for it later. Although at the time, I was happy not to learn. I made my life a little harder. Father was right; I did need to know those things. Unknowing the error I was making, I made life hard for my poor auntie. I would never have had the fortitude to stay and work with such awful children. She must have been a very tough and an understanding lady. I never even got to know her well.

Auntie Ruth was a wonderful cook and seamstress. She made the finest lace for dresses and curtains, even very fancy tablecloths. All of it was made with a tatting shuttle. She worked so quickly your eyes could hardly keep up with her hands. Auntie Ruth also made and mended clothes for all of us. It was a great help to mother. Mother made things for us as well, but never with the fine and straight stitches of Auntie Ruth. Her seamstress skills were an art. She made our old clothes look fancy with flower and bird patches. She really cared about us and made horse patches on my clothes. I don't think I ever thanked her for all the work she did for us.

I watched the men doing rope work and axe work. I

The Story of Two Alaskan Children Growing Up Wild

learned from them to splice ropes, make halters, split wood, notch logs, fell trees, and all other jobs more suited to boys. It was really a blessing in later years when I had to cut firewood and run pack trains for father. I guess it all worked out fine. I was more enamored with wildlife and wild living.

Johnny and I had plenty of time to explore and find trouble to get into. We rode our ponies at a run every place we went. If we weren't on the ponies, which was rare, we would be running our own legs off. Spring days encouraged us to go a lot farther from home. A burlap bag or two was always tied to our saddles to hold whatever we found or caught as we rode through the hills and valleys of our mountain home. The bags were usually full when we returned to the homestead. Full of what was always a question.

Early in June, we spent most of a day catching baby ducks, which were put in a bag to take home. We were quite proud of ourselves. Mother made us take them back to the lake after a good dressing down about them being wild birds that couldn't live in our chicken yard. The next day we brought home coyote pups. Mother didn't think much of that either. We had pretty much the same result as the previous day. We had to find something mother would let us keep. We found the only animals mother let us bring

Johnny & Me

home were fish and game we could eat. Thereafter, we spent more time playing than getting food. When we did bring home fish, squirrels, or birds, they were only for eating.

That spring our older sisters hooked four donkeys to the old hay wagon. The wagon was in sad repair and had no bed; only some boards nailed together that lay on the old bed support. They only had a rope tied to the halter of each lead donkey. I guess that helped to stop them since they didn't rein at all. Our sisters had Johnny and I fill two fairly large wooden boxes with small rocks. The rocks were used to make the donkeys move and to turn them. Johnny being very good in his rock throwing (having had a lot of practice with our other livestock) would throw rocks into the opposite side when we wanted to turn. It actually worked rather well, and soon he only had to throw one rock at each turn. Father was not that impressed with us, and put a stop to it when he caught us. Father may have been a bit premature on that though, as the donkeys were much better behaved afterward.

Before father caught us, we had a couple of weeks of fun. Those donkeys took us everywhere the road went in our valley. We had a little trouble going down hill. Good thing the hills were not too tall as the wagon picked up

The Story of Two Alaskan Children Growing Up Wild

speed and nearly ran over the donkeys on one of the steeper hills. There were shafts, but you could still jack knife the wagon and have quite a wreck. Going home was easy though as any hills were all going up. We were quite a sight to see I am sure, six children with two boxes of rocks and three dogs all sitting on four boards in the middle of that donkey drawn wagon. I don't recall meeting anyone on our trips except on the last ride, when we ran into father coming home from the mountain. I might add running into father was pretty much what happened. That wagonload spooked his packhorses, and they ran away bucking and leaving most of his supplies in the road. Father was yelling at us and trying to keep control of the pack string he was leading. I found out that day we were all a bunch of idiots and didn't have the brains god gave a goose. Well, I guess I had been told that before, but maybe not quite so loudly.

    Needless to say, we all shared in the picking up and hauling home of everything that had been left in the road by the bucking pack string. Everyone walked home leading the donkeys. The wagon was now piled high with five horses' packs in various degrees of damage, mostly just dirty. So

Johnny & Me

ended our wagon rides, but not to worry, we were only to think up other adventures.

The Story of Two Alaskan Children Growing Up Wild

Maple Syrup Town, created by the Luster kids

CHAPTER 5

Father had a bottle of whiskey or rum that he added to his coffee sometimes. He always shared with any person that was visiting. He called it, "Coffee Royal." There was

Johnny & Me

one exception to father's generosity. He was afraid of the traveling preachers seeing a bottle of spirits of any kind in the house. One day he happened to see what he thought might be a preacher. He yelled, "Hide the whiskey here comes a preacher." The nearest person to the bottle happened to be my oldest sister. She grabbed the bottle and stuffed it down in the couch cushions. Only she never screwed the top on. The smell was obvious immediately upon entering the house. Father shouted for mother to take the cushions out the back, and he grabbed two chairs and went out the front to sit on the porch.

When the preacher drove up to the house, father invited him to sit with him on the porch, as it was such a nice day. Mother soon brought coffee out and joined them. After all the pleasantries were taken care of, the preacher had all of us on our knees out on the porch while he prayed. I don't know what he prayed about, but I do know he took his time. After a while Johnny and I sneaked around the corner and got out of there. No telling what the preacher would think up next; he'd probably be dipping us in the lake or something. That had happened before with a different preacher. I don't know how many of our sins were washed away the first time, but I wasn't taking any chances. Just in case this preacher saw a few sins the other preacher

The Story of Two Alaskan Children Growing Up Wild

missed.

Johnny and I made our escape out the back and ran for it through the horse pasture. I bet father wished he could have followed us. We climbed the big hill and lay under a nice spruce tree and took a nap. It was a nice warm day after all. We didn't come home till we saw the preacher drive off down our road. Nobody missed us I guess, as nobody said anything about it when we returned. Father just put us to work cleaning out the tack shed. We didn't clean it very well; mostly, we just played. We found some cans of military C-rations. We opened up a can and ate what was in it. It wasn't very good, but we were hungry. Cold C-rations kept our backbones from touching our belly buttons. I think we lost interest in cleaning the shed and wandered off to play a short time later, which was what usually happened. We were the champions of half-finished jobs.

It seemed we had a lot of preachers prowling the woods for people to save that summer. Not to many days went by that one didn't show up. It seems to me; it was always about suppertime they showed up. Mother would just put on another plate and told us never to let anyone go away from your door hungry. If all you have is soup, then add more water and cut the bread slices thinner.

One day a man showed up on our homestead. He

Johnny & Me

was a hobo I think. Mother sat another plate for him as well. After the prayer the hobo reached into his boot and took out a fork and spoon. He said there was no need to get one of mother's dirty. He pulled a bowl out of his coat and used that to eat in. We were very interested in what else he may have stored about his person. Turns out, he had quite a few things. He carried everything he needed in a pack or in a pocket. He showed us all the neat things he had. There was a double-back knife sharpening stone, which he used to sharpen all of mother's knives. Screws and washers to fix pots and pans. He had a small axe wrapped in an oiled-cloth and many other odds and ends he used to fix things for his supper. He even had some wonderful stories for us children. We all were sad to see him go two days later.

Johnny and I took to carrying things in our pockets and a small bag that we might need. We decided that when we grew up, we would be hobos as well. It sounded like a wonderful and exciting life. We spent many hours making plans on where we would go. Maybe we'd go to China first to see the Great Wall. There were so many places we had read about that it was going to take a long time to see them all. We stored things we might need for our future trips in our fort. I think mother lost a few pots and pans to our hobo dreams.

The Story of Two Alaskan Children Growing Up Wild

We lost interest in becoming hobos about halfway through the summer. There were far to many things that happened every day, which sent us down new and unexplored paths. As our father was a hunting guide, we saw many different people from many different places. Each person had something new to tell us. We always were full of questions. I'm sure we got on everyone's nerves. Most people will talk to children and tell them stories, or at least that is how it worked for us. With each new story our plans changed on what we were going to be when we grew up. There seemed to be many choices, which gave us many games to play and even more plans to imagine. We spent many hours making lists of what we were going to need in the future. I'm sure we wasted a lot of father's precious writing paper. No one ever said anything about it though. I think mostly because we shared a lot of our plans with father. He even joined in and gave us new ideas of what may be needed for our journeys. I think he was having as much fun as we were. He advised us not to wait too long. In fact, maybe we should start by next spring.

Mother never thought much of father's ideas though. She told him not to encourage us. We could think up enough trouble on our own. Mother said maybe we should learn to cook and bake a little. What a great idea! Johnny

Johnny & Me

and I decided to make cookies as our first project. This entailed bringing in enough wood to keep the cook stove burning several hours. That didn't take too long and didn't distract us from making cookies. Mother had to let us make the cookies, as she had given us the idea in the first place. Mother did not help us at all. She said we were on our own.

When asked how to make cookies, she just told us, "well it's kind of like making pancakes." We put flour, eggs, salt, baking powder, and milk in a bowl. Stirred that up then added 2 cups of sugar. Mother gave us some raisins. We put one in the very middle of each cookie, making sure it was well covered so as not to get hard and black. Each pan of cookies was watched carefully, so they would not burn. We had made a lot of dough, and it took a long time to cook all that batter. We cooked late into the evening. Everyone liked our cookies, and so did we. Johnny and I sat behind the stove where it was warm, eating cookies. The last batch of cookies was in the oven, and we were very full and sleepy. It was nice and cozy behind the stove. Too cozy in fact, and we soon fell asleep. You would have thought the smell of burning cookies would have woken us, but nope.

We woke early in the morning because we were cold. As we passed the table, we noticed a plate full of cookies. They looked like charcoal bricks. Mother had arranged them

The Story of Two Alaskan Children Growing Up Wild

very nicely on that plate. Even added a cup of milk. We stopped and shared the milk. Then went on to bed. No one ever said a word to us about the burned cookies. When we got up later in the morning, the cookies were gone. Mother knew we had seen them since the milk was gone. That was a lesson learned. We had wasted food. That was a very serious crime, and we knew what it was like to have any food. We decided we were done with the cooking and baking for a while. Time to find something new, preferably something we were good at.

    We found several gallon cans of paint in the trash pile of one of the neighbors. It had been thrown away because it had been frozen and was really in bad shape, but it was just what we needed to fix up our fort. There was a can of yellow; one can of blue, and two cans of white. We put the four cans of paint in two burlap bags and hung them on our saddles. We found an old mop and some rags in the trash as well, which we used as our paintbrushes. After riding the mile or so to our cabin in the woods, the paint was opened, and we began our project. The paint was really thick and had big dry lumps in it. I guess it made our log walls textured. We painted until we ran out of paint. That was probably a good thing as we were more painted than the logs. I think we could have been invisible when standing next to the walls. Camouflage! But, our fort was really beautiful now.

By the time we got home, our saddles and bridle reins were covered in paint as well. After all, it was oil-based house paint. At least we could not have fallen out of our saddles; we were pretty much stuck to them. Father saw us ride in and had a laughing fit. Mother was not quite as impressed. She made us scrub with turpentine. That was not fun at all. The paint didn't come off easily. We had paint on us for several days, not to mention the raw spots from scrubbing with the turpentine.

Getting the paint out of our hair was a project that mother had to do. Mother cut Johnny's hair pretty much down to his scalp. I was another story. After mother was finished with me, my hair was a lot shorter and a lot thinner. Mother cut my bangs all the way to my forehead. My eyes burned for days and were bright red from the turpentine. There were blisters on my scalp too. Most of my eyebrows were missing. Johnny's eyes and eyebrows had not fared much better. I think we looked like a couple of rabid moth-eaten squirrels. I don't really care for the smell of paint or turpentine to this day.

After we were washed up, we still had to clean the paint off the saddles and bridles. Even with father

The Story of Two Alaskan Children Growing Up Wild

supervising us, all the paint never came off those saddles. They kind of had a pale blue hue to them for years. They were little kids saddles and pretty beat up anyway, so really no one really cared. I think they looked better too. No one would steal them after that either because we'd recognize them. So, it was all good in the end, at least to me anyway.

Johnny and I didn't go back to our cabin for quite a while. The paint had plenty of time to dry. In fact, I don't think we went back that year at all, as it was time to go to the mountains to clean hunting camps. That was a job needing to be done every year. Pits were dug for any leftover trash. Corrals were repaired along with hitching rails and any fence that had been broken down by moose. Moose were the worst fence wreckers. They don't even take notice when they run straight through it. Sometimes, they can take out a quarter mile of fence and never get a scratch. This is not the case with horses. Horses seem to get cut up even looking at a fence at times.

The cabins and tents had to be cleaned and repaired also. The porcupines and squirrels always chewed up everything. Johnny and I spent a lot of time trapping the fat little ground squirrels. Mother would put eight or ten squirrels in a large Dutch-oven pot with onions and potatoes. After cooking in the coals for a few hours that was

Johnny & Me

some good stew. We also spent time looking for porcupines. The big ones taste kind of gamey, but with plenty of garlic, we never complained. Johnny and I spent a lot of time fishing as well. There were a lot of trout in the rivers and streams near the hunting camps. I never cared for the grayling we were caught. They have scales that have to be scraped, and we had to clean all our catches before mother would take them. Sometimes, that was a lot of fish to clean. On the plus side, we kept mother supplied with something to cook. Luck was with us, and on two occasions we brought back to camp little silver porcupines. Mother fried them up, and they were wonderful, much better than chicken.

At most of the camps, there was some food because father would bury small barrels of supplies, mostly dry goods like flour, sugar, beans and rice. There was always salt too. Sometimes it was rock salt, but that works just as well. To complete a meal, we really just needed meat. That was what Johnny and I best at providing: fish and hunting small game.

The older girls were busy fixing camps and running horse pack strings between camps. They liked to fish and hunt also. They were just too busy helping father to get much time for it. They would sometimes stop to fish

The Story of Two Alaskan Children Growing Up Wild

between camps if they were hungry. They'd cook the fish on hot rocks by a campfire. Sometimes they'd stuff the fish with berries, mushrooms, or fresh mint that grew along the creeks to give it a little different flavor. Small game was cooked pretty much in the same way.

There are usually enough edibles along the trails to keep a person from starving in summertime. Some of the edibles don't taste that good but were eaten anyways. We chewed a lot of spruce gum. It didn't taste good either, but after a while of chewing it, the spruce taste went away and then it was good to keep your mouth busy. Everyone was always happier when my mouth was busy doing something other than talking. The soft end of grass that is pulled out of the stem is also good to eat. There is always Labrador tea growing in the mountains that can be brewed. I've always liked it. No reason to go hungry with food all around you. Of course that depends on the season. In winter, it's a lot harder to find things to eat. There's always fish, if you can get through the ice.

Porcupines don't taste to good in the winter either, as they eat spruce bark, but they are easy to catch. If you are hungry, you'll eat them despite the taste. They make good dog food too, as dogs don't mind the taste. Porcupine has to be cooked even for dogs, because they carry

Johnny & Me

parasites. Food doesn't have to taste good if you are hungry. I remember there were times we even ate the horses' oats. Cooked they aren't half bad. A little chewy, but it fills the empty stomach. I guess you get plenty of fiber too. I am pretty sure the food we had back then was better for me than the prepared food people buy in stores today.

There was a lot to do in the mountains: hunting, fishing, hiking, and looking for gemstone. Everyday we would climb one of the mountains. Johnny always got to the top first. He would wait for me at the top, but he never had to wait to long. We would sit on the top and look over everything below. We'd try to sit on whichever side didn't have a wind and listen to the marmots whistle. We loved watching the wary little pica rabbits. Sometimes, if we were very still and the wind was just right, the white Dall sheep would surround us as they grazed. As soon as the sheep got our smell, they were gone, leaping over the rocks and ledges. They would dart quickly, taking their lambs at dangerous speeds over the cliffs. None ever fell, though I always feared for those little lambs.

On our last climb before leaving the camps, we went to the tallest mountain there. After topping out, we were looking down on two mountain goats napping below us on a ledge. They were only about ten feet from us and couldn't

The Story of Two Alaskan Children Growing Up Wild

smell us, as the wind was blowing toward us. We sat and watched them for quite a while. They were watching all about them, but never looked up. It was probably close to an hour went by before one of us got restless and moved, breaking a small rock loose. Those goats jumped straight up and fled around the ledge. We went down where they had been and looked around. Hearing a rock above us we looked up to see those two goats were now were we had been, looking at us. They just stood up on the skyline and watched us make our way down hill. I guess they thought we were no threat, just two small children. That was the last time I ever saw mountain goats on that mountain range. They were all hunted out in the years to come.

That was also the last summer all our family was together. It was 1959. Times were changing for us, although we didn't know it yet. There was still plenty of summer left, and plenty of fish to catch and squirrels to trap before winter. Johnny and I were happy to be free in the mountains. We were always ready for new adventures.

Johnny & Me

Mother, Fay, Stella holding Johnny, Hilda, and Bonnie

CHAPTER 6

Our oldest sister Lucy had gotten married that summer. She was 16 years old, and soon after getting married, she was expecting a child. She had married a man that did part-time

The Story of Two Alaskan Children Growing Up Wild

work for my father. He was about 28 years old. We thought he was an old man. She lived down the road about a mile. Well, not much of a road, mostly a dirt track that went to the lake. It was just a tiny two-room log cabin. She really kept it clean though. I guess she never had a lot to do there. She was trying to make a home for the baby she was expecting.

Her husband worked in Anchorage, which was seventy-five miles away. He didn't get home every night, mostly just on the weekends. She was alone in that tiny cabin in the woods. I guess marriage didn't seem quite as wonderful as she had expected. She would walk over to where we lived most every day. That is until her husband bought her a little flatbed truck.

After she got that truck, she would fly down those old dirt roads. That truck must have had only one speed: fast, because I don't ever remember her going slow. I don't know how she kept it on the road. Everyone started calling her Lead-foot Lou. Thankfully we never worried about getting run over by her, as that little truck had stacks up both sides of the cab, and you could hear her coming two miles away.

She gave us a ride home one day in the back of that truck. Once was enough. There was nothing to hold onto except the hot pipes in the back. We almost flew off several times. Screaming at our sister to stop and let us walk had no effect. We lay down as flat as we could in the bottom of the bed and spread out. That kept us in till we got home, but just barely. My belly was bruised black and blue from pounding over the bumps. Johnny was not in any better shape. Walking seemed to us a much safer way to get home. Thank the Lord we only had a couple of miles to ride back there. I don't know how my sister drove that truck down that rough road so fast being pregnant. It could not have felt good. She never slowed down though, so I guess she was just tough.

Lucy's husband also had a motorcycle with a sidecar. That way he could bring home whatever was needed from Anchorage town when he came back from work. Many things were brought home in that sidecar. One late night we were awakened to my brother-in-law's knocking. Turns out, he had brought home a fairly large pig. How he got it to ride the 75 miles in that sidecar, I will never know. The pig none the worse for the ride was put in our pen to fatten for winter.

Johnny and I had more than one ride in that sidecar. We were small and could both fit in the seat at the same time. The rides were always scary. At least for me, but we always wanted more. It was like a scary carnival ride, terrified while you're there but thrilled afterwards. 1969 was

The Story of Two Alaskan Children Growing Up Wild

also the year we moved from our home. Father made plans with my sister's husband and another hired hand to move to a very remote mountain about three hundred miles away.

After selling our land and most of the livestock, father bought a tractor-trailer rig to carry all our belongings and what horses we had left. There was somewhat of a road to within fifty miles of where we were to go, but it ended at a river. We would have to cross the river with horses and go the rest of the way with pack trains. Father wanted to be farther away from civilization. There would be no school there, as we would be the only family within fifty miles. Father liked to be away from other people. He did not like civilization. I guess it choked him.

Two weeks before we were to leave, father and the other two men had a falling out. I don't know why, but we never moved to that valley. As our home was gone now, and we had no place to live, father moved us to a small cabin on the banks of the Chickaloon River. I mean right on the bank of the river. The river was no more than twenty feet from the cabin. On the plus side, we didn't have to carry water far. Our big stove was gone, but it didn't matter, it could not fit into that cabin anyway. Mother now had to rely on a big five-gallon copper boiler on the stovetop for hot water. It was the job of Johnny and I to keep it filled. We

Johnny & Me

carried small buckets from the river each day, as it needed filling. We got tiring after a few weeks of carrying the small buckets, so we decided to just carry the boiler down to the river and dip it in and carry it back. It seemed like a good idea at the time. If mother had caught us, she would have stopped us. To bad she wasn't there.

We got it carried down to the river as it had handles on each end. It was built perfect to do this job we thought. Apparently, we were not built for the job. We dipped the boiler into the river and that was the end of it. The river current took that boiler on a one-way trip to Cook Inlet. We tried to get it back, but we couldn't go in the river, or we would be joining it on its trip. We ran along the bank for quite a while hoping it would snag on something. Sadly, it never did, and now we were in big trouble. Running away seemed like the best thing to do.

A note was written to mother. We explained how we had lost the boiler, and that we were very sorry we would not see the family again but this was the best way. After packing a few things in burlap bags we saddled our horses and headed for the mountains. Apparently, we were not that good at planning. We figured the best places to run away to were fathers hunting camps. After all, they had just been fixed up for hunting season. There was plenty of food and

The Story of Two Alaskan Children Growing Up Wild

shelter. Little did we know, we were heading into more trouble.

We went to the nearest camp. It had a nice cabin and plenty of feed for the horses. It was a lot of fun staying there. We ate canned fruit and fished a little. Hunted rocks and trapped a few squirrels. Life was good. Well, it was good for about three days. The morning of the third day we found that our horses had run back home. It had also begun to rain. Thankfully, there was a stove in the cabin.

The next two days were spent keeping warm and taking turns bringing in wood. That wasn't so bad until a rather large bear showed up. We couldn't go out to get any more wood, as we were afraid the bear would eat us. The cabin cooled off in a couple of hours. Night came and so did our fear of the bear's return. We tried to be quiet and only talked in whispers. We were dry, and that was the only good thing we could think of.

Late in the night, the door jerked open. I am sure I must have half crushed Johnny getting up in the rafters. Somehow Johnny got past me and was perched as far as he could get in the apex of the roof. There were a few boards laid across the rafters. That's where Johnny and I were hiding when father got into the cabin. He never said a word, just lit a lamp and proceeded to bring in wood and build a fire. After a while he put on a pot and started cooking some rice and raisins. We watched him set out 3 bowls and three spoons. When the rice was ready he filled the three bowls and sat down to eat. He stated loudly, "this is some mighty fine rice, I guess I'll have to eat it all myself. Seems you two kids don't want any." We bailed out of those rafters, scrambling to sit at the table. That bowl of rice and raisins sure did taste good. It didn't take us long to get to the bottom of the bowl. Everything was good now. There was nothing to fear any more. There was no bear born that could get past our father.

After we had eaten, father asked if we were ready to come home yet. Before we could answer, he said we could think about it until morning. Mother sure could use our help. Everyone would be sad to lose us, but they'd understand about us wanting to live up here by ourselves. Mother would probably cry, but the little girls would be glad to have extra room in the bed.

Of course we would have to move out under a tree when he had hunters there, as he would need the cabin for them. Maybe in the winter when he was trapping he would need it again, but other than that we could live there. If we kept a fire going, it would keep most of the bears and wolves away, though maybe not the big ones. They seem to

The Story of Two Alaskan Children Growing Up Wild

break into cabins even when people were living there, but we would probably be fine.

I don't think we slept very much the rest of the night. Mostly we whispered about what to do. We didn't want to appear too eager to go home, but home was where we wanted to go. Morning came early, and we were up before father and had the horses caught and tied to trees. We noticed father had brought our ponies back, and our burlap bags were packed.

Father baked some baking-powder biscuits and fried some potatoes for breakfast. He never said anything about us going home. Just talked about the weather and how it was going to get cold up here now. It would snow soon, as it was higher in the mountains. Johnny and I just saddled our ponies and tied on our bags. We were not staying a day longer up there. We didn't want to make mother cry, and we would be glad to share a bunk with the little girls. That is what we had decided as our reason for going home. A bear might have had something to do with our decision to go home, but the hot meals were pretty nice too.

When father closed the cabin door, we were already in the saddle waiting to ride home. Nothing was ever said about the loss of the copper boiler. Mother had a large round galvanized tub to heat water when we got back. It had to be filled every day. We were back to packing buckets from the river. Never did we think about trying to carry that tub to the river. I think we had finally learned something, although it was a hard lesson.

We were put to washing clothes with a washboard and doing the dishes almost every day. We always had to haul water first. That pretty much kept us out of trouble. Mother needed us to take up the chores of the older girls, as they were now working for father in the mountains most of the time. It was time for Johnny and I to take on more responsibility. We were growing up.

I helped mother make the lye soap from the wood ashes. It was hot work and took a lot of time, but it had to be done before it started raining again. The messy sludge was poured into pans to dry out hard. After the soap was dry and hard, mother dumped the pans and wrapped each loaf in wax paper. The soap was stored in a wooden box until it was used. Mother put sage or lavender in some of the soap we used to wash our hands, but it still smelled like lye to me.

The Story of Two Alaskan Children Growing Up Wild

Johnny and Mike, the dog

CHAPTER 7

It was fall now and time to pick as many blueberries as we could. The best berries were twenty miles away at

Johnny & Me

Puritan Creek. That is where we were going today. The mothers from the Chickaloon Village came to get us. They had two cars and a truck. All the children rode in the back of the truck. It was quite nice with sides and a tarp over the top. Blankets and sleeping bags were piled inside, as well as many buckets and baskets. We stayed warm and comfortable, and most of us slept on the drive. The babies rode in the cars on their mothers' laps. This was not just a berry picking expedition. It was also a time for sharing and learning.

It didn't take long for a camp to be set up. There was a small cabin there for the children to sleep in. Tarps were laid out to cover the dirt floor. Sleeping bags and blankets were thrown on top of the tarps. It would be wall-to-wall children inside. We would be warm. A nice fire pit was not far from the door in front of the cabin. Some of the mothers started a fire and began to prepare a supper. Everyone else went to the berry patches. Even the little ones went to pick berries. Well, some of the little ones were picking the berries out of the buckets and filling their bellies. It was a wonderful time. I must admit I ate my share before filling my bucket. It did not take long to fill a five-gallon bucket. The berries were large and abundant. The children had small pails that when full were dumped into the five gallon buckets. Soon there

The Story of Two Alaskan Children Growing Up Wild

were four big, five-gallon buckets of berries.

We could all smell the fry bread cooking, and it was enough to bring everyone back to supper. The children were sent to the creek to wash, the little ones helped by the older children. Only a little whining could be heard now and then. There were some nice, big rocks set around the fire for use as chairs where it was warm, leaving room to walk. Every child was given a big piece of fry bread. We all settled down and waited to be served our dinner. It was mostly the fry bread we wanted anyways. I don't really remember what we ate for dinner, but after dinner we roasted marshmallows. The marshmallows came in a box with the words "Campfire Marshmallows" on the side. They were kind of hard, but softened up when heated over the fire.

After everyone settled down around the fire, it was story time. Each mother took her turn telling us lesson stories. Everyone enjoyed the stories even if we never learned anything. The younger children soon fell asleep. They were carried off to sleep in the cabin soon followed by the rest of the children. The blankets were warm and all were asleep almost before our bodies hit the blankets.

The morning came with the smell of blueberry pancakes. It didn't take the children long to get out to the fire for breakfast. Blueberry syrup had been made. With

Johnny & Me

butter and the syrup on the pancakes, it was a feast. The older children were put to work cleaning the campsite. That was a quick job. Then they were off to pick more berries. It didn't take long to fill all the available pots, pans, baskets and buckets. All to soon, it was time to go home. Everyone lingered around the lunch fire talking and drawing out the time, reluctant to start home. The fire was drenched, and a walk around the campsite to ensure everything was cleaned up meant we were finished. Nothing was left behind. It was left as nice as we had found it, for the next person. Our little caravan headed home much richer in berries as well as our hearts.

There would be a lot of jam and jelly made as well as syrup. It was much needed for our winter food supplies. Mother even canned some berries to use in cakes and pancakes. We had some jam on biscuit's the next morning for breakfast. After a couple of days our mouths were getting sore from the acid in the blueberries. All the children looked like aliens from the staining of the berries and the sores around our mouths. We were all tired of eating the berries anyway. Mother made all the jams and jellies she could, sharing berries with the homestead wives that lived only a couple miles away. Mother always shared any extra we had with others. Mother even shared some berries with

The Story of Two Alaskan Children Growing Up Wild

the old "Crazy Fin" man across the lake. I guess he made wine with them. He made a lot of wine when he wasn't building boats. Maybe that was why he was called "Crazy Fin." He did make some really nice boats though.

That old man did not like children. He would yell at us every time we played in the lake. Sometimes he would chase us with sticks. Of course we could out run him quite easily. He thought we were getting the water dirty. Maybe he should have run off some of those ducks, geese, and muskrats. I think they put a lot more nasty stuff in the water than we did. The lake was quite large anyway, and we only played on our end, which was a good half-mile from his side.

The lake was full of small bullhead fish we could catch with our hands. After building a fire, we could cook them in old tin cans. Frogs were added as well. They were small but if you were hungry enough, you could catch a lot of them. Sometimes we could catch some land locked salmon in the side creeks that ran into the lake. Those were a lot better and didn't have sharp spines. Those little bullhead fish tasted mostly like mud, but they filled an empty stomach if you caught a lot of them. We did catch a lot of them. It saved us from going home, and we could play all day and all night if we wanted.

Johnny & Me

The Fish and Game Department eventually poisoned out all the fish in the lake. I think they were trying to poison the leaches. The leaches were the only thing left when they finished poisoning the lake though. That put a stop to all our fishing in that lake. To this day, it still has no fish in it. It's very sad. We tried to transplant more fish from the river and lakes in the area, but the fish didn't seem to take hold. Maybe the leaches ate them? Frogs still live there.

There are a lot of other lakes in the area as well as the Chickaloon River; so, we still caught plenty of fish. We just had to walk or ride a farther. We didn't mind most days. In fact, we liked to be gone from home as much as possible. That way we could do what we pleased, which we did mostly anyway. Life was good for two adventurous children.

The Story of Two Alaskan Children Growing Up Wild

Aunt Ruth and Grandma Luster

CHAPTER 8

It seemed we were like the animals that lived in the mountains and valleys with us. We fattened up in the summer and thinned down in the winter when there wasn't as much food available. The food didn't completely run out most winters, although it did happen a few times. Mostly, if we didn't have anything else, we could shoot a moose. Moose seemed to winter near wherever we did. I guess that was nature watching out for us.

Things never got to bad when father was around. He just was gone for long stretches at times though. Hunting and trapping took a lot of time and work. Getting paying hunters took a lot of time also. Father had to travel to other states to meet with prospective clients. That took months away from home. Those times could be a little tough.

Father moved us down to Old Matanuska that winter. It was the town site preceding Palmer. There were only five or six houses still standing. Most of the old boardwalks were rotted and gone, leaving only nail-studded boards here and there. We used the old boards for kindling. It gave us extra wood and cleaned the area up. Leaving them lying around was just a hazard for people and horses. We had a lot of bare foot children, and the horses ran free around the town, if you could still call it a town.

Auntie Ruth moved there with us. She took up residence in what had been a general store. It was the next largest building left standing. We moved into the largest building. I think it had been a restaurant or bar. It worked

The Story of Two Alaskan Children Growing Up Wild

out for all of us. There was even room for our big table in the front room next to the kitchen. It was the biggest house that we had ever lived in. There was a separate room for father and mother. The hall and pantry became bedrooms, as well as the back porch. There was a room behind the kitchen that made a bedroom for the four youngest children. This was a great house. There still was no running water, and it was still outside plumbing. We did have electric lights though. That was really something. Also, we only had to walk a few hundred yards to catch the school bus.

It would have been even better if the moose didn't winter there by the hundreds. We were a little afraid of the moose, as they would chase us and try to trample us to death. It was always a game of hide and sneak. We must have been good at it though since no one ever actually got trampled. Some of the dogs did because they would bark at the moose and try to chase them. Moose don't chase, unless they are the ones chasing.

Life was a little different for us there in Old Matanuska. Johnny and I could walk or ride a horse to the town of Palmer. It was not that far. We found friends to spend time with. Two boys lived only a little over a mile away. Another boy lived in town but spent a lot of time at our house. Having friends everyday was the greatest part of life. Sometimes, we would ride to town and bring our friend, Harry, home with us.

His mother always let him spend time with us. We spent a lot of time at his house too, mostly because his mother fed us. She was a really good cook. She was also a fast cook and could have something made in a hurry. We never went away from her door hungry. Sometimes, she even packed us something to eat on the way home. We didn't really need any thing, as it was only about eight miles to town. We would run our horses most of the way to or from town, at least ride at a fast trot.

Sometimes we brought a horse for Harry, most of the time he just rode behind one of us until we got home. We usually rode bareback. Bareback was better when it was cold, and it was cold a lot. Not as cold as in Chickaloon, because Chickaloon is at a higher elevation. Cold is normal for Alaska after all. The wind seems to blow a lot more often and a lot harder in the Palmer area, which is more coastal. The weather never seemed to bother us one way or another. Except if it was below zero with 50 mph winds, it would keep us inside more. We found things to do in the wind as well though. We made sails on our sleds and wagons, depending on the snow level. There was no steering, but we had fun until we would end up in a bush or over a bank. I

The Story of Two Alaskan Children Growing Up Wild

guess that was fun too, in an exciting way.

Sam and Steve lived up the hill from us. They could ride hand sleds or bikes most of the way to our house. If they came on a sled, when it was time for them to go home we would tie a rope on the sled and tow them back up the hill. They got a pony or a dog tow depending on the snow level. We used a pony a lot because the snow didn't stay as much there. They only needed dogs when the snow was deep. Sam and Steve had a bird dog that was quite large named Sac. He towed the sleds home many times. Mostly they would tie the sleds to Sac and let him tow them up the hill. They walked. It would have been too heavy for Sac if they rode the sled.

Sac was a good dog and pretty smart. I don't know how well he retrieved birds, but he was a great protector of those boys. Nobody could come close to those boys without Sac's permission. More than a few people were chased away by that dog. We all loved him. He was warm to sleep with too. We spent a lot of our time fishing in the Matanuska slough. Salmon as well as trout swam there. We ate a lot of fish. In fact that was mostly what we had to eat, rice and fish. Father always bought a lot of rice. It kept better than potatoes. It could keep for years if kept dry. There are not many ways to cook fish and rice. Mother tried

Johnny & Me

them all. Fish stew is not good either unless you are hungry. We were hungry a lot.

I think we would have had a lot more hungry days on Old Matanuska if not for Sam and Steve and the salmon they caught. We helped catch fish as well, but those boys were masters at catching salmon. We stacked up salmon like cord wood under the house so the game warden wouldn't see them. There were way too many of them to be legal. It was freezing under the house. This made for dog food as well as people food. We were all happy to have salmon for winter food.

Sam brought a pair of hip waders down to our place to keep from getting wet while fishing the slough after it turned cold. He let me wear them. They were too tall for me, but I did wear them. Wading in the slough was a lot of fun. Sam kept telling me to watch where I waded because there were deep spots I could fall into. I was not careful where I waded and soon stepped in over my head. I will tell you hip waders are not good to swim in. They also do not come off easily, as they are strapped to your belt. I couldn't get out of that deep spot and was well on my way to drowning. I was climbing the sides under water, but not really making much progress when suddenly a hand grabbed me by my braids and pulled me up. Thank God for Sam. It was a cold walk

The Story of Two Alaskan Children Growing Up Wild

back to the house. I never complained, nor did Sam, and he was just as wet as I. It was my fault that he was wet, but he never said a cross word to me. He just seemed to be happy that I had not drowned; so was I.

Sam never complained about anything. He was always in great spirits and seemed happy to share company with anyone. My father was always quite fond of him. Of course that may have been in part because Sam always jumped right in and helped in any work that was being done. He also didn't talk too much. Talking too much was something father did not like. Maybe that was why he wasn't overly fond of my company. I couldn't keep my mouth shut for five steps. I was also very argumentative.

Father always told me my mouth would get me in plenty of trouble in life. That seems to be true. It seems I always gave my opinion, even if no one wanted it. It can cause people to be gun shy with a person. What a winter we had at that place. Father sealed the porch in with visqueen plastic to make a green house. With the windows open, it stayed warm enough to grow tomatoes and squash among other things.

Mother was pretty happy to have a few fresh vegetables available all the time. Well, maybe not at all the time, but enough to have an extra green onion or tomato to add to a stew or roast every few days. Green tomatoes were good also. Father spent a lot of time in his green house when he was home. I guess he could be by himself and still be warm. He had put a chair in there, and mother would hand him a cup of coffee through the window.

Father was home more that winter than I ever remembered. He did a little trapping on the tidal flats for fox and small fur. I think he was crushed from not moving to the mountain valley, as he had wanted. As spring approached, his mind moved on to new plans and of course beaver trapping. Father would take one of us to help on his trap line. I loved when it was my turn. We took the dog team on a circuit and would finish out the line coming back from a different angle; that way we could cover more miles in a day. It was fast runs between traps. The more traps that were full took longer time to bait and reset. Sometimes the area was torn up after a full set. The traps would be pulled and put in a bag in the sled. They had to not touch anything or they could get bad scent on them. We would hurry between places, always happy to see a full trap. Sometimes we would take a side trail to set a new group of traps and snares. The dogs needed to be held away from where the trap sets were. A tree or big log was good to tie off on, if there were any nearby. Mostly, I would just hold the lead

The Story of Two Alaskan Children Growing Up Wild

dog until father was done.

We were rewarded with a lot of fox that season. Mostly red fox, but we also got several cross fox and two silvers. There were enough ermine to trim out several pair of mukluks. We even caught a couple dozen coyotes. As spring was upon us, we started the beaver and muskrat trapping season. It starts in February. Beaver trapping is hard work, as you have to chop holes in the ice, and then plant poles in the bottom of the pond. The ice can be a couple of feet thick. It is still cold and your hands get really wet. Drying your hands and getting them back in gloves is of the utmost importance. Not doing so can cause frostbite and the loss of your fingers.

Beaver was very important as we used the meat for dog food. The entrails were used for bait, and the tails mother cooked with beans. There is nothing like a big bowl of beaver tail and beans. The last thing we trapped was muskrat. They were easy because when days get longer, they push up their houses from the marsh. This is why their homes are called muskrat push-ups. To catch a muskrat, you just set your trap on top. Easy money. Well, they aren't really worth a lot of money, but you can catch a ton of them in a day. Fifty to seventy-five cents apiece is pretty good money when you can catch a hundred rats in a day. Of course, catching so many meant we were busy skinning and stretching hides. When they dried on the boards, they all had to be removed, sorted, and graded. Mother usually did that. It was all a lot of work, but we never noticed.

The spring is not too long in Alaska, and being busy made it pass even faster. We went to bed tired each night and woke ready to do it all over again. Money was good that year, even with out the larger fur animals. Father was able to get good prices for the fur and bought plenty of supplies for summer.

It was time to repair all the horse gear, wash and oil all the saddles and harnesses, and re-strap the pannier boxes as needed. We also need to braid snaps on lead ropes and rivet buckles on anything that needed it. Every saddle blanket needed to be cleaned and dried. I guess you could call it our version of spring-cleaning.

The biggest job was cleaning the dog lot. There was a lot of raking, shoveling, and hauling dog waste. It was a dirty job, but it had to be done. The doghouses had to be cleaned and repaired as well. At least we didn't have fleas in Alaska. Johnny and I got the job of cleaning out the doghouses, as we were the oldest of the little kids.

School was still open, and we worked after school and on weekends. There were a lot of dogs, and they

The Story of Two Alaskan Children Growing Up Wild

weren't our only chores. It took us a week to finish the houses. It was a lot easier to feed and water the dogs now that we didn't need to watch where we walked as much. That was one of our chores as well, not the walking, but the feeding. The barn needed mucking out as well. It seemed there was no end to the jobs that needed to be done. At least that was my feeling.

The foals needed a clean place to get out of the weather. The hay also had to be stored inside. Even the chickens needed to be in a clean place. They made nests in the hay; so every day was an egg hunt. If not found the day they were laid, the eggs froze. Frozen eggs made extra dog food.

Petting the foals was something we all liked. I spent a lot of time in the barn playing with the babies. I was not the only one though. The foals were all halter-broke by the time they were a couple weeks old. They were well handled and petted often. They were even used to us putting fingers in ears and nostrils. We made little rope harnesses and taught them to drive. That was how our horses became good, steady, gentle, and useful horses when they grew up.

Johnny & Me

Johnny in a pedal car

CHAPTER 9

As we cleaned the yard, all the rest of the boardwalks were torn up and burned. We found a lot of cool stuff under the boardwalks like old bottles with bail tops, an old watch that of course didn't work, and my sister's boyfriend even found a ruby ring. He gave it to my sister as an engagement

The Story of Two Alaskan Children Growing Up Wild

ring. She was almost seventeen, he was twenty-nine.

My sister was married shortly after that and moved to a tiny house a little way away from us. I think it was really a shed, about twelve by fourteen feet long. It was big enough for a small wood stove, a small gas cook stove, and a bed. They built a crib in the corner for the baby when they had one. A small table fit in the cabin as well. I have no idea where they kept their belongings, maybe under the bed. Mostly they ate with us, since we had a big wood cook stove, and mother could use the help.

Another sister one year younger than the last one, married about a week after. She was sixteen years old. This one moved away to Chickaloon with her husband's family. Mother didn't have to cook every meal now and could do other things. She made a lot of quilt tops and flour-sack clothes for us. The flour came in fifty-pound cotton bags in print patterns. We had shirts and dresses made from them. We thought they were beautiful. I guess they were. Mother had a treadle sewing machine by then, and Auntie Ruth helped with sewing. That old sewing machine sang away many of the days.

Auntie Ruth made lace with her tatting shuttle. Our flour-sack dresses had beautiful lace collars. My older sister even helped crochet lace for our clothes. Auntie Ruth showed my mother and sisters how to make sewing patterns, as she had been a dressmaker in Wyoming years before. My sister made all her own baby clothes. I think they were better made than the clothes you get in the stores now days. They were sewn with love.

Auntie Ruth set up a quilting frame and worked to finish all the quilts. Everyone had new quilts even the neighbors. Now, we actually had blankets on our beds. That was really something nice. No more sleeping bags. We still didn't have any sheets but used two blankets instead. It was wonderful.

We were getting more civilized all the time. We still lived a primitive life, but we were closer to town and had an understanding of how others lived. Our manners were improving, and we were cleaner. Not quite the savages that we had once been. Even my hair was combed more often. My clothes were cleaner, and I had got a better handle on my mouth. It was progress.

The Story of Two Alaskan Children Growing Up Wild

Father and Johnny, hamming for the camera

CHAPTER 10

Now with three sisters gone to husbands, my father was short of help. Johnny and I became the new wranglers and pack help. We were small and had to work harder at doing our jobs, which we did. Johnny and I rode the thirty miles to Chickaloon leading a string of nine horses each. They were tied head to tail. We had to keep them lined out so they didn't block any cars or truck when we were on the road. The bridges were the worst part, as we had to actually walk on the highway to cross them. Most of the way we went along the pole lines. Some of the way, we had to return to the highway as the pole line went over cliffs and across rivers. We did fine and got all the horses up to summer pasture in good shape.

Though we were only nine and ten years old, we were not afraid to stay with the horses until father arrived a few days later. Father pulled a couple candy bars from his pocket, and I was excited to have one. Johnny and I were at the point of having eaten very little and starving. Pretty much, at that point even mud pies would have been good.

That was the start of our summer. It was feast or famine the whole summer. We were sent from place to place with the horses so they would be available for father. The life of a wrangler was a summer of adventure. Rivers were crossed, and mountains were climbed. A lot of time was spent spotting where game was hanging out for later hunting.

Father specialized in guiding for Dall sheep and grizzly bear. Climbing mountains for sheep was fun. All the

The Story of Two Alaskan Children Growing Up Wild

hunting camps had to be cleaned and stocked for fall hunting. We had spring hunting and summer fishing trips, as well. We were always busy. Fishing was still my favorite pastime, as I could fish with the client. There's nothing like fishing. Well maybe eating the fish, as it's pretty good too.

There was always fun to be had, even when it rained. Games and challenges were part of the hard work. We see who could get across the swollen creeks and rivers without having the horses drag us out. It was fun until father caught us. Father didn't think it was fun, and we both got a good lecture on the dangers of crossing high water. We may have gotten a boot in our behinds too, but we were on the other side of the river, and father didn't want to cross it. Across the river is where we stayed until the next day, and then the river went down. We had no supper that night, but at least our horses had grass. It was actually a good lesson to learn only losing our dinner, as people drowned in that river even with a horse.

We trapped and shot the pine squirrels around the camps because they chewed up anything they can get into. They also taste good and made good stew. Nothing really went to waste. Father always planted a few veggies at the main camps. He usually planted carrots, onions, and some potatoes. Occasionally, he'd plant lettuce and cabbage.

Johnny & Me

When we came back in the fall, the vegetables came in handy. Sometimes moose would come and eat the cabbage. Moose will eat an entire garden if they find it. Even a fence doesn't keep them out. Usually we didn't plant cabbage as moose can smell that for quite a ways, and they love cabbage.

We would weed the little gardens each time we passed them during the summer. Father had to plant a lot of carrots, as we would eat them as soon as they had a little size to them. Fresh carrots are wonderful. We usually had fish for breakfast most days, as we could drop a line near most of the camps. Getting up to fish was no hardship. In the summer in Alaska, we have a lot of daylight, and it is hard to sleep anyway. Besides, children don't need much sleep when there is fun to be had. We'd have plenty of time to rest when we died is what my father always told us. Good advice I think.

Johnny and I stayed in the mountains alone most of the time, doing what needed doing. Father would drop in to wherever we were once in a while. On one of his trips back, he brought our friend, Harry. What a great surprise! Harry made the rest of that summer even better. We had a lot more fun, and had even more adventures. Some of those adventures scared us.

The Story of Two Alaskan Children Growing Up Wild

One of us thought riding logs down the river to camp would be a faster way to bring in the firewood. We found out Johnny swims like a rock. Between Harry and I, we got him out only half drowned, and that ended that idea. Not to worry, there were three of us to think up bad ideas. Believe me, we did just that. No one was hurt badly during the whole summer, which was pretty amazing. Looking back, I think it wasn't due to anything we did but rather pure luck we never got seriously hurt.

For a short while we camped near the Glen Highway close to a roadside lodge. Johnny got the idea to give horse rides to tourists. Actually that worked out pretty well, and we had money to buy burgers at the lodge. We all came out of that experience with a couple hundred dollars. It was great. It was the most money we had all summer. Our hunter tips didn't even top it. We got to keep all that money too. Father never even got mad at us for using the horses. Instead, he told us that we did good. It was probably the most praise we'd ever got from father in our whole lives.

Mother sent in some candy bars for us. They were all chocolate. I don't like chocolate, but the boys liked them just fine. I was pretty pouty for a few days when they pulled out candy to eat it. It was all good though, as in the next

Johnny & Me

camp I found two cans of spinach. I love the stuff; it's better than candy. I've loved spinach since I was four years old. The year I was four, our house burned down, and we had to stay with some missionaries. Spinach was served one night with dinner. The other children were whining about how they hated it. I joined in with them, saying how much I hated spinach. The lady missionary asked me if I had ever eaten spinach. Well, I said no, but if it was as bad as everyone said, then I didn't want any. She told me I should taste it first, and see what I thought. Maybe I would like it, maybe I wouldn't, but I should try it for myself before I decided. I tried it, and she was right. I loved it. That was a lesson I have applied to the rest of my life in many areas. It was a good lesson.

A lot of squirrels were trapped and hunted to keep them out of our hunting camps and for eating too of course. Porcupines were always on the menu if we found the little silver ones. The big porcupines don't taste very good, even in the summer. They eat too many spruce trees, and the spruce flavoring is in their meat, but we would eat them if we couldn't find anything else.

There were enough warm and sunny days to make summer fun. We fished and played as well as worked. We even panned a bit of gold when we had time. There was a

The Story of Two Alaskan Children Growing Up Wild

lot of gold when we were in Caribou Country. There isn't much gold there now, as big mining companies dredged every creek and river in the whole drainage. We got a few ounces of small nuggets by the end of summer. We stored it in toothbrush cases that we buried under rocks. Unfortunately we forgot what rocks we buried it under and at what camp. We never found it again.

Harry Buzby and his mother

CHAPTER 11

In midsummer father sent us home for a few days to see mother and get some fresh clothing, as ours was getting pretty worn out. We had made enough money with our horse riding enterprise to go shopping at the department store in Palmer. It was called Koslosky's. We all got Levi 501's and new shirts with pearl snaps. We were looking pretty fancy in our outfits and new boots. We also got a couple of blue work shirts. The fancy shirts were for town and church. Mother made me wear a dress for

The Story of Two Alaskan Children Growing Up Wild

church, so my new shirt was for town trips. I hated dresses. In those days you had to wear dresses to school. I didn't like that much either, so I would wear jeans under my dresses.

We didn't go back to the mountains for a couple weeks and were enlisted to help mother and the little girls with whatever needed doing around home. There was a lot that needed doing, believe me. I think there was more to do at home than in the camps. There was less time for play at home. Winter was always on my mother's mind.

Old Polly, our horse, was used to drag logs home for winter firewood. That actually was fun for us. We would hook a log to the chain and climb up the harness and ride her home. Quite a stack of logs was pulled behind the house. I don't think much of it made it to wintertime, as mother was always busy canning and drying stores for winter. Cooking and canning take a lot of wood. A lot of baking was also done. Mother made cookies and fruitcakes that were put away. I loved mother's fruitcakes. She used real fruit and berries she had dried. The cakes were wrapped in wax cloth and put in the root cellar. They lasted for months.

Water was hauled in dairy cans on a stone boat, which is a flat bottom sled that was pulled by Polly. There

Johnny & Me

was a lot of water to haul with all the clothes to wash and pens to clean. At least mother had a gas washing machine now. She'd traded up from her old washboard; praise the Lord. The little girls did most of the dishes now. We were the hands now and had outside chores to do, but garden weeding was hard work for everyone. At least you could eat carrots as you worked in the garden that is unless mother saw you.

Winter was always on everyone's mind. It was coming, going, or already here. We were always preparing for it, or cleaning up after it. Winter was the one constant with everything in life, and mother reminded us daily. Soon, it was back to the mountains to work for father again. This time we had rock hounds as customers. We were packing these guys in to the mountains to only pick thunder eggs. Father had a claim on a huge thunder egg bed. Johnny and I had a lot of free time to fish while the clients picked over the rocks they wanted to haul out. We had fish to take out with us too, as we caught so many. Father would smoke any extra fish when they got to the homestead.

When the clients were satisfied with their pickings, we packed up the horses and brought them out. We each had two or three packhorses carrying rocks tailed to our riding horses. The packs had to be rearranged every few

The Story of Two Alaskan Children Growing Up Wild

miles because the rocks shifted with every river and hill. One of the packhorses fell on a hill and the thunder eggs rolled all the way to the bottom. Those rock hunters were not happy and made us bring every rock back up that steep hill. Johnny was madder than I was about it. We hid some of the rocks under bushes rather than bring them back up. Today there are thunder eggs in places they never were before, and it's no geological mystery. It was Johnny and me.

It took two days to get out of the mountains with that pack train. The first day we only went as far as the cabin. One of the horses had to be traded as he had worn a sore on his shoulder from the packs. Father greased him up with some kind of salve and turned him loose out on the mountain pasture. There were several horse left at the cabin camp. The extra horses stayed on the meadows all summer to be used as needed. They had bells on to make them easy to find and keep the bears away.

Hauling those rocks were hard on the horses, as they shifted so much the packs would ride wrong and bruise the sides of the packhorses. We had to stop and adjust the packs every few miles. This made getting home take a lot longer. We salted our fish that night so they would stay good and be ready for smoking when we got home. It was cool enough to hold them until we got out. If they went bad by the time we got home, father would have thrown them in the dog food cooker. Nothing was wasted. We cooked up rice and raisins for dinner with brown sugar and a little butter.

    It was pretty good, but I'm not sure those rock hounds thought so. I love rice any way it's cooked. We eat it a lot, almost every day in camp since it is easier to pack than potatoes. You can get a lot of mileage from a bag of rice. It goes with everything you could find to cook. Eventually we did get home, and what a relief that was for everyone. We were all tired and hungry and glad to be back.

    Mother served us a great dinner with buns fresh from the oven to soak in the stew she had simmering on the back of the cook stove. I ate so much I fell asleep in the corner behind the stove. It was nice and warm behind the stove with the heat reflecting from the copper sheet nailed to the wall. The copper was put there to keep the wall from getting too hot and catching fire. Later in the night, it cooled down enough that I woke up chilly and made my way to bed.

    The morning came early with bright sunlight shining through the windows, heating up the room. Time to get up and start chores of some kind. First, I just wanted to go out to stretch and breath in the freshness of this day. I loved to

The Story of Two Alaskan Children Growing Up Wild

watch the birds fly about and listen to all the morning music of nature. What a wonderful life we lived, there in the back woods.

The smell of breakfast cooking took me back to the house. I liked to eat. I wasn't particularly picky about what it was, just so it filled up my belly. Usually breakfast was pancakes and syrup, that mother had made, with eggs on the side. By the time I made it in to eat breakfast, everyone else was already at the table eating. There was a plate for me on the stove. Mother just smiled when I seated myself at the table.

It was back to home chores again. Chickens, goat, dogs, and the garden all needed something done. If we hurried, there would be time to fish at the lake. Feeding chickens and goats was pretty easy and fast. Mother had already milked the goat and picked up the eggs early in the morning. We checked for eggs twice a day, as they were checked when the chickens were locked up for the night. The dogs were the most work. Their food had to be heated on the fire pit. Today it had been done in the early morning as well. We were off to weed in the garden for a couple hours.

The garden had more weeds than should have been there. I guess our trips to the mountains were making more work for everyone that stayed at home. The little girls didn't spend that much time in the garden I guess. We pulled weeds for a while, just lost in our work. Seemed like it wasn't that long before the little girls came out to get us for lunch. After washing up, we went in for a lunch of chicken soup and bread.

The soup had big, homemade noodles. That was the only way you got noodles back then. I never saw store bought noodles until much later in life. Homemade noodles sure made better chicken noodle soup than anything you can buy from a can. Sometimes, mother made dumplings instead of noodles; they were a lot faster to make and really good to eat.

The afternoon was ours. Johnny and I disappeared off to the woods as soon as lunch bowls were washed. We had to get out of sight first; figuring out what we would do would come later.

We each had a rope to catch a horse and use as a war bridle. We went into the field for a horse, and away we went. We decided to go up the mountain to look at a cave that needed exploring. When we got close to the mountain, there were huge swamps we had to go around. Some swamps we got through by jumping from grass clump to grass clump. One of our horses got stuck for a bit, but we

The Story of Two Alaskan Children Growing Up Wild

worked it loose and continued. It took a lot longer that we thought it would. We tied the horses at the bottom of the rocks and climbed to the cave. The cave was a place where the sheep and other animals came to lick minerals. The licked and licked until a huge over hanging shelf that was about fifteen feet deep and forty feet long had formed. It was deep with sheep and goat manure. It was dry though, and it didn't stink too much. We sat on the ledge in front and talked for an hour or more before we realized it was getting late.

After hurrying down to the horses, we walked them up to the coal mine and rode back on the mine road. It was well after dark when we got home. Dinner was over, and we had missed it. Not to worry though, mother had saved us a small pot of stew and hard biscuits. The biscuits soften up just fine once I soaked them in the stew.

We told mother about the mushrooms that were up the hill from us and that the blueberries were getting ripe. A plan was made to pick mushrooms the next day and blueberries in the next week. Mushrooms would be dried or canned. Drying those type mushrooms is not easy as the bugs lay eggs in them if they are left out to long uncooked. They are very tasty in soups and really good fried in butter. Alaskan countryside always provided for us.

Johnny & Me

It was more than a week before we went back for blueberries. It was just the right time to pick them. We took the horses, one with a packsaddle and the panniers. Both panniers were filled as well as a couple of 5 gallon buckets with lids that were hung on the saddle. A lot were picked and eaten. Blueberries are perfect right off the bush. We saw one bear eating berries as well, but thankfully not very close to us. It was on a slope about a mile away. Everyone had a lot of fun and did a great job of getting blueberries for mother's jam.

The next couple of days were spent cleaning and cooking berries for jam. The tops of the jam jars are filled with paraffin wax to seal them. I liked chewing the wax like gum, then eating it. It made mother angry with me for wasting the wax she needed to can that jam, and it got me kicked out of the kitchen and sent into the garden for weeding. I liked it outside better anyway. We would all be grateful for the jam and syrup that was made later in the winter. For the next two days we ate blueberry pancakes with blueberry syrup for breakfast. After about a week, we were all kind of tired of eating blueberries.

Preparing for winter is what took up most of our time. From spring till winter came again. It was always about winter. We seemed to work continually putting up hay and

The Story of Two Alaskan Children Growing Up Wild

feed for the livestock and fattening pigs, goats, chickens, ducks, and geese. We also worked in the garden, and forested mushrooms and berries and anything else that we could find to store up for those winter months. We had to find a way to make all we needed in the short summer months or go without it in the winter. Most of our lard was made from bears, because we didn't have pigs every year. A lot of grease came from geese, which was excellent for cooking. Even our soap was made with lard and ashes. Not a lot of stuff came from town except the dry goods like flour, sugar, salt, and canned fruit.

Our whole family had to work together to survive. We were raised to be self sufficient and responsible. We were all able to drive a teem of horses, hunt, trap, and cook a meal. We were forced to grow up tough and self-reliant, but growing up was the main thing. It was a hard life and some kids never got the chance to grow up. Looking back, the fun we had growing up wild was worth the hardships by far.

That winter was bitterly cold, and the snow was deep. We moved back to Old Matanuska with the horses. They could feed there on the swamp grass. The wind kept the snow in drifts, leaving the grass mostly accessible for the horses. They had to dig for a lot of it, but not so deep. The horses stayed fat and happy in spite of the winter snow.

Johnny & Me

There was a slough where holes could be chopped open each day for water. That was one of the chores I had to do.

At Old Matanuska, we were back where we could see our friends almost daily. We would go to their house, or they would come to ours. It was only about a mile to one friend's place, and only eight miles to town where the others lived. It was all within walking distance. Of course we had school as well. This was uptown living.

The railroad tracks were just a short ways away from our house. We played a lot in the rail yard. There were sidings were the work trains stayed. Railroad crews lived in rail cars parked there. We got to know them and visited there regularly. They were all nice guys and gave us treats and books to read. They had a nice wood stove in their boxcars that kept it warmer than our house. Sometimes they shared meals with us, which was not a way to get rid of us.

There was a shed where they kept supplies in on the side of the switcher. Johnny and I got some of the track explosives and ice picks from the supply shed, as it was not locked. The explosives were used to warn trains to slow down in case of track problems. Johnny and I clamped them on some of the tracks and watched the trains run over them. Wow, did we get in trouble for that! The railroad shed

The Story of Two Alaskan Children Growing Up Wild

was locked after that. We felt bad for how we had repaid those men who were nice to us. We were ashamed, as we should have been. After that episode, we stuck to putting pennies on the track to flatten out. That was fun too, but not as explosive. I think I may still have a couple of those pennies somewhere.

We walked the tracks a lot to go places, because around Old Matanuska there was a lot of swampy ground and the rail bed was high and dry. The railroad trestles got us over the rivers we couldn't have crossed even with horses. I decided to lead my horse over the Knik trestle like I had read in a book. I had a little girl from town with me. We only made it out over the water before the horse fell with his leg stuck through the bridge beams. I climbed under the tracks and pushed his leg up while the little girl pulled on his reins. After pulling his leg up, he fell over the side and into the river. The little girl went with him. All I could do was jump in after them from under the bridge. It was not as high a jump as they had just made. I got the little girl and held onto the horse's tail as he made it to shore and drug us out. We had to explain what had happened, why we were wet and why she had lost her glasses. No one cared that we almost froze to death on the way home, or at least they didn't care that I had almost frozen to death. I was in deep

Johnny & Me

trouble. The biggest problem was I had taken a town kid with me, when I was being stupid. The event taught me just because I read something, doesn't mean I should try it. We really could have died from my stupid idea. Luckily the horse didn't break a leg, as that would have been a terrible thing to happen. I guess mother was right, "God watches over idiots."

During the winter, a railroad car that was carrying feed spilled on the tracks. One of the work crew walked up to our house to see if we wanted to salvage the grain. Yes, we did. We hitched up a horse to a big sled and started hauling the feed to barrels in a barn close to our house. It took us most of a week to clean up that spill. We had grain for the whole winter. What a great score, thanks to the railroad workers.

Some moose found what little grain we couldn't clean up and stayed there for several days. One of the moose got hit by a train and was made into dog food. I guess it all worked out; the train wasn't damaged. Mother started cooking grain in the dog food. Along with the moose meat, it was pretty good food for the dogs.

With all the feed the horses had, they were in great shape all winter, and we could ride them without over working them or taking too much weight off. Ride them we

The Story of Two Alaskan Children Growing Up Wild

did. We went everywhere on horseback that winter. Spending a lot more time in town, as it didn't take as long to get home. All the farms around us were in reach now. We visited everyone that we knew and made friends with the ones we didn't know. Soon we had more friends than we had ever had in our lives. Of course, it didn't hurt to have horses the others could ride. I think that is really why most friends spent any time with us. Others really were our friends. It didn't mater either way; we were having a great time. What a great winter we had that year.

But, not everything was great. There were still plenty of chores and responsibilities to do each day. The snow was deep and the wind blew just about every day. The woodstove took a lot of wood, as it was a barrel stove and couldn't be shut down very well. We dragged in wood from wherever we could find it. Most of the trees in that area are kind of small. Weekends were when we cut most of the wood, dragging it home with horses from sometimes a mile or more away. We always had to be careful to watch out for moose that wintered around the area.

Hundreds of moose wintered on the tide flats as the snow blows the ground bare enough for them to get around to the willows that grow there. Moose browse on willow and birch twigs. They also eat the swamp grass and plants that are abundant and easily available in the area too. The moose don't seem to like horses any more than they like people. Moose will charge and batter horses that they think are too close to them. Cow moose are the most aggressive as they are protecting their calves.

The moose wintering on the flats has kept most of the willow and birch trees small and bushy. Only the trees in the middle of patches of brush have any size at all. The snow drifted and packed hard in the brush, making it difficult for moose to get too far into the bushes. That is where we had to find firewood. Most of the trees were small birch and cottonwood. Every now and then, we'd find a dead black spruce. Finding the spruce was a real good thing, because it was dry, and we needed it to get the birch burning. Dried spruce is the best fire starter. The cottonwood was not desired at all, as it burns quickly and didn't make much heat. It also leaves a lot of ashes that need to be cleaned out, but we got whatever we could find. We burned it all, because we had to. When the firewood was cottonwood, we found it took a lot more of it, which meant a lot more cutting and hauling. We didn't have a chain saw, only a bucksaw or Swede saw, as it is also called. It was hard work, but we were tough and sometimes our sister's husband helped. He had a chainsaw and would

The Story of Two Alaskan Children Growing Up Wild

saw up logs that we drug in. We still had to split the rounds, but that was the easy part.

It was hard to get to the haystacks sometimes, as moose were standing or lying near the hay yard. They would fight the horses off the hay, if you didn't get it spread out enough for everyone. The moose seemed to grow in numbers more of everyday. One morning, I counted seventeen moose laying in the yard between us and the outhouse. Not a good situation. I don't think our outhouse got much use that morning.

My sister's husband shot the cow moose that had been giving us the most problems. She was nice and fat and tasted delicious. Eating that one moose made us all not so mad at the other moose. The moose kind backed off after that. It wasn't so scary to be outside, which made life easier.

Christmas wasn't much that year as we really didn't have much money. We did have a nice big moose brisket roast. Mother made a great meal for us. Our older sisters and their families came to share the day with us. It was a wonderful day for everyone. We were blessed.

School photo

CHAPTER 12

Winter vacation was here. We made the most of every day of it. Skating on the slough took us for miles from home. We just had to be careful of open water as the tide comes up that slough, sometimes breaking the ice, and

The Story of Two Alaskan Children Growing Up Wild

then covering the holes with a thin sheet of ice. We never did fall in, although we sometimes got wet feet from the overflow on top of the ice. If that happened and we were to far from home, we had to make a fire in the nearest brush and dry out. That was no hardship for us. We always looked for horses while we were out. Some we hadn't seen since they were turned loose for the winter. By the time we had to return to school, most of the horses were accounted for. There were three we never saw again. Luckily, they were a crippled mare and two colts. Maybe wolves ate them. It wouldn't be the first time.

All the horses we found were fat and healthy. Some we brought back home to use in place of the ones we had been using all winter. The other horses needed a break. Two of the mares were in foal, so they couldn't be used for pulling anymore. We started using a couple of big half draft geldings: one grey and one roan. They made an excellent team. We could pull two sleds chained one behind the other. That made our woodcutting a lot faster. By the time vacation was over, we had a large pile of logs behind the house. We wouldn't have to cut wood for quite a while. We would still have wood to split, but that wasn't so bad.
We had dogs to use as well as horses for traveling. The dogs were a lot more trouble to use, as there were nine or

Johnny & Me

eleven dogs to harness and handle. With the horses, it was only one or two. Sometimes the snow was just too deep for horses or when it was going to be a fast run, the dogs were used. We ran the dogsleds down the ice or on trails that were open. We could make a pretty fast trip with the dogs, even to town. Going to town on the shoulder of the road was dangerous, as speeding cars hit any dogs that step too far into the road. That happened to my sister's husband. A car hit one of the dogs dragging the rest of the team into the road, killing three of the dogs and wrecking the sled. Luckily, no person was killed, although our brother-in-law was bruised up and very angry. His lead dog was one of the dogs killed. It was also his favorite dog, more like a pet. He couldn't race again until he trained another leader. Our dogs were no good for him as ours were freighters, while his were speed dogs for racing. He used one of our leaders just to train a new leader for his team. He didn't win any races that winter, because his new leader was too green.

One of my sisters raced dogs when she could. She used the fastest dogs we had. They weren't fast enough though, and she never did that well. Once she got the red lantern for being last in a twenty-five mile race. It was a little red coal oil lamp, and she was pretty happy with it. She said at least she got a prize. I was told that the reason she was so far behind was because her lead dog saw a moose and left the trail to chase it. After chasing the moose for several miles, she finally got her tired team back on the trail and finished the race.

She won a couple of women's races, but never any of the open races. She always finished though, even if it was late into the night. Some races were long ones of over a hundred miles. There were spotters all along the trails for safety.

Race days were fun like a carnival. There was always coffee and cocoa. Sometimes there were cookies and donuts. The mushers' wives brought the desserts. That was before someone started selling food at the races. The best part was the races were held on the flats near where we lived. We could just walk right over to the start lines. Johnny even entered some of the kid races. He actually won some as we worked our dogs every day, and they were well trained. We also knew the trails well, as we ran them frequently.

Years later Johnny ran in the first two Iditarod races. He was always an athlete. He didn't do well in those two races as his dogs got sick in the first one, and he got sick in the second one. Moose were a big problem for mushers. They would trample a team of dogs if they were on the sled trails. Several teams lost dogs for this reason. Mushers began carrying guns to scare the moose. If that didn't work and the dogs or mushers were being attacked, they could save the dogs and themselves by shooting the moose. The Troopers would be called, and the meat salvaged to be given to someone that needed it. Sometimes, it was us. If we got the meat, we would haul it home with the sleds. You had to have signed up for meat salvage or just be in the right place at the right time to get a moose. They still have a meat salvage program today in Alaska. It's called the road kill list. You can put your name on it by October, signing that you will respond when called any time day or night to pick up a moose or caribou that has been hit. Usually night as that is when most of the moose are killed on the road. You need to be there to pick it up within one hour. It is best to get there while the Troopers are still on the scene, as it is dangerous to be on the road without flashing lights in the dark.

Any moose or caribou hit on the road or railroad is available for salvage. Sometimes the animal is good, but a lot of time the meat is too damaged to use. Usually when a train hits a moose, there is not much left. Sometimes though, they are thrown clear and are very good condition for salvage. Our family always was always on the salvage

The Story of Two Alaskan Children Growing Up Wild

list.

Leaving the gut piles lying near the road is not good because coyotes, foxes, eagles, and other animals are killed while scavenging. When you get one of the moose from the kill list, you should pull the gut piles as far from the road as possible or take them to a dumpsite. If we got a moose near the road, we always took the whole moose away to prevent further wrecks and more animals killed. This system of salvage has helped a lot of people survive through the winter. A moose is a large animal and provides a lot of meat. It can really make a difference to hungry families.

Winter was coming to an end, things were thawing, and there was plenty of mud. It was break-up time, the ugliest season of the year. Break-up leaves no secrets. Everything done in winter is soon revealed. Cleaning up is a lot of work. Everything from saw dust piles to dog poop has to be removed from around the house. There was a lot of both that winter. Nobody wanted to track it into the house. If you did, mother would be very unhappy, and sometimes we were chased out of the house with a broom. The muddy dogs as well.

It would soon be warm enough to move back to Chickaloon. Everyone was ready to get back to the mountains. We only needed the snow gone and the grass to start growing again for the horses. When that happened, school was over for us. We just left and stopped going to school, as once in Chickaloon, we couldn't get to the road to be picked up at that time of year. We had learned enough that school year anyway. There were a lot of things to do on the homestead.

Mares were having their foals and had to be kept near the house in shelter. This meant feeding and cleaning up after them. The hay we had put up the year before, now came into use. All the horse came home from the pastures in the mornings for hay. The grass wasn't very abundant yet. Hay was forked over the fence near the house. It had to be done quickly, so the horses didn't kick and bite each other. There were a couple of bullies in the bunch that would try to hoard all the hay if the piles weren't far enough apart. It was good not to be in the fence with them too. They would run over or kick anyone in their way. Things would mellow out, as the grass came in better. The horses were just hungry.

Father was putting shoes on all the horses at the rate of two or three each day. He had a shoeing chute near the corral. They were tied to a solid post in the front of the chute and locked in behind. Bars on the side were used to hold up their feet while father worked on them. Father was a top-

The Story of Two Alaskan Children Growing Up Wild

notch farrier. Most of the horses were worked in that manner. We had a couple that had to be thrown and tied down to work with their feet. One of those was the best kid's horse we had, called Old Smokey. You just couldn't mess with his feet, or he'd go crazy with fear. He would bite, kick and rear up striking out with his front hooves. Father threw him on the ground and had one of us sit on his neck. His shoes went right on with no problems that way.

Smokey had bit and kicked father before and one time broke his wrist. Father was not taking any more chances for that to happen again. After all, the horse weighed in at 1200 pounds and father was only 130 pounds. Father was a very good hand with livestock. Spent his life with horses and knew how they thought. He knew how to use a rope and could tame and train the wildest horses brought to us. He used to say it was easier to train the horses than the people that used them. We were taught if you trained a horse with kindness you could always trust that horse, because the horse trusted you. Where as a horse broke with fear would abandon you at the worst possible times. I have found this to be true in my dealings with horses through the years.

After the horses had their shoes on, they were turned out for a while to get used to the feel of trimmed and shod

Johnny & Me

feet. The spring trimming took off a lot of the hoof and changed the angle of their pasterns. If you used the horses right after shoeing and trimming, there was a good chance they would go lame. During the summer trims, it didn't matter if you used them right after being shod and trimmed. Their feet were kept short in summer and fall but not in winter. Sometimes, we didn't see the horses till spring.

Some of the mares with foals and small ponies didn't need shod, only a trimming. Father shoed all the horses he was going to use first. The rest of the horses were done last. No shoes meant a quick run through the chute for trimming and then back to the pastures. He finished up the rest of the herd in about 2 days.

It was time to take a break. That afternoon we made a big fire at the lake and had a swimming party. The neighbors showed up with hot dogs and marshmallows that were roasted over the fire. Someone made Kool-Aid for all the kids. It was a lot of fun for everyone.

I didn't swim that well, and Johnny swam like a rock, straight to the bottom. We stayed on the edge in the shallows and spent our time catching little bullhead fish and trying to keep the leaches off. There were black leaches and green ones. Some of them would be six to eight inches long when stretched out. They are pretty disgusting. We chased

The Story of Two Alaskan Children Growing Up Wild

the little kids around with them until some adult caught us and put a stop to it. It was just for fun, but the adults didn't see it that way. We stayed fairly late in the evening until the mosquitoes sent us all home. What a good lake party that was.

We were short on meat so it was time to go fishing again. Now that was a job I could really get into. All that was needed were three horses saddled with burlap bag tied behind the saddle and fishing poles stuffed in the gun scabbards. Since Harry was along, we gave him Old Molly. She was a good horse but slow. Johnny led the way, and off we went.

There were sea-run rainbow trout in Saw Mill Creek back then. The fish were easy to catch in that creek as it had beaver dams all along it. We just fished in front of the dams. There were pools that weren't too deep; others we couldn't see the bottom. Johnny built a fire down stream just before the pools. We would cook a fish or two when we got hungry. We took turns fishing and tending the fire.

After a couple of hours, we had caught a bunch of trout. Most were ten or twelve inches long, but we caught a few bigger ones of over twenty inches. It was pretty exciting to catch the big ones, although they didn't fight as hard as the smaller ones. We were after food after all, so it was

Johnny & Me

good to get the big ones. We cooked up a couple of the smaller ones on rocks by the fire. Fishing was fun, and we took our time heading back. Soon enough we headed home, as people at home needed to eat as well. When mother fried the fish later with coating and spices, they tasted much better than what Johnny and I had cooked. Our cook out had been good too though, but it wasn't the flavor, it was being out on our own with our friend that made it seem so good.

The Story of Two Alaskan Children Growing Up Wild

Johnny with a grizzly bear he shot

CHAPTER 13

At the beginning of summer, both Johnny and Harry had bur haircuts. A bur haircut is a style where the barber basically takes a razor to your head and shaves all the hair down to less than an inch long. I wanted one too but was not allowed. It really wasn't fair. Hair does grow back you

Johnny & Me

know. Braids were all I was allowed as usual, so I got out my pocketknife and made them very short braids. Wow, was I in trouble after that! I didn't care, but my older sister had to get out the scissors and straighten it out. She made it even shorter, to even up the places where I had cut closer to my head. In the end, I was happy with my haircut. It was more of what I wanted anyway, and it was better than long braids. Besides, my sister told me it would grow out again. While that thought gave her comfort, it didn't give me any.

With my hair short, it was now easy to wash. I only had to dip my head in the water and dry it off like the boys. By the time school started we would all have longer hair. Well, I wouldn't have braids any time soon, but I liked that. My new haircut was just in time to be in style. The pixie was now popular that school year, soon to be followed by the shag. In my case, it was just shaggy.

The only bad thing about our haircuts was the mosquitoes. Too bad they didn't make hoodies back then. The mosquitoes loved ears for some reason. Right away, I could tell I should have left the hair a little longer there. That summer, both Johnny and Harry had sun burned heads covered with mosquito bites. They kept scratching, which didn't look very good.

At least hair washing was easy now. The boys just

The Story of Two Alaskan Children Growing Up Wild

had to a wet cloth swiped over the top. I could wet my hair while washing my face, such an improvement in time and cleanliness. Mother should have been happy with me. After all, she always wanted us to wash up and have clean faces, but she was not. Mother never said much more about my haircut, but the looks she gave me could curdle milk.

Father had traded for a small motorcycle that he gave to Johnny. It was a Honda 50. It got a lot of use that summer, going places I am sure it was not designed to go. I rode with him quite a lot. Good thing we were both small, not 150 pounds between the two of us. Johnny took us everywhere on that bike. Going to town was fast now. Gas didn't cost much, especially with the low fuel usage. We did wreck quite often but really didn't get more than road rash and scratches. Usually the wrecks were on horse trails. We were not going fast in the woods, but sometimes faster than trail conditions merited as sticks and rocks were part of most of the trails. Usually, we'd wreck by flipping over after we were caught by one of those sticks or rocks. Maybe I should call them flip-overs, as the bike wasn't damaged, and neither were we. A few more scrapes and bruises fit right in with what was already there. Who would notice a few more? I am pretty sure if mother had known she would have curbed us in some way, but maybe not. She always told us to be careful. We tried to be careful, but getting down the trails and roads as fast as possible was not easy. At least the bears stayed away from us on the bike. They could hear the motor from miles away. That was good too, as it is a lot safer then surprising bears on the trails.

It was not easy to carry much more on that bike than the two of us. I started wearing a backpack, which helped. The backpacks in those days were a lot bigger than what is made now. We didn't call them backpacks either; they were packsacks. The trouble was if you put to much heavy stuff in your pack, it would put to much weight on the back tire causing instability in the front, thus, more wrecks. Sometimes horses were just better transportation.

On the trails, horses were not much slower than motorcycles. Horses were much safer and didn't scare the game away. But for Johnny, they weren't as much fun. Horses and motorcycles didn't work well together either. If you were behind the horse on the motorcycle, you couldn't get past on the trail unless there was a very wide place. You risked getting kicked off your bike, if you got to close to the backend of the horse. If we came to an open meadow you could go around. Father didn't like the bike on any trip we made. Johnny got yelled at a lot, but it never made a difference in his taking the bike. Father was always yelling

The Story of Two Alaskan Children Growing Up Wild

Johnny was scaring the game clean out of the country. He was right about that. That still didn't stop Johnny until Father finally threatened to get rid of the damn bike. The bike was used pretty much only on the roads after that. Johnny only had the bike for one year as I recall. Just wore it out from all the abuse I guess. Johnny probably got more use from that little bike than most people would have. A car seemed to be the next item of interest, but a car didn't come any time soon. Although Johnny saved every penny toward the purchase, it just didn't work out for him. Things always came up that needed money. Johnny always spent his money on things that mother needed.

Maybe it was for the best at that time that Johnny was not on the roads with a car. He tended to speed a lot. Hitting a moose or even a bear was very much a road hazard. Having been in the car when this happened twice was pretty scary; at least no one was hurt. Both the bear and the moose that were hit were killed. Well, the bear had to be shot, as it was still alive and badly wounded. Both cars didn't fare in the collision. We butchered both the moose and the bear, so they were not wasted. Meat was never left to ruin. Father made sausage from the bear. I guess that ended well. Bear sausage is some pretty good stuff with eggs in the morning.

Johnny & Me

Although Johnny repaired the little bike many times, it finally was beyond repair, and we were back to horses and walking. Not for long though, as father decided to send Johnny to a ranch in Wyoming to go to school. Johnny was excited for a new adventure; I was not so happy. Father thought I would do well going to a Catholic school in Copper Center when winter came. We had a month before we would leave. We had to make the most of it. Who knew when we would see each other again? That turned out to be a couple of years. Nothing was off limits now. We swam the horses across the lake and fished almost every day. Staying out in the woods and cooking whatever we caught or shot every night on a campfire. Eventually, we had to get ready to leave. We rode with our older sister and some of our cousins in a camper. I was to be dropped at the convent on their way out of state. All of us kids rode in the camper with no way to talk to the people in the truck. This turned out to be a bad thing.

After driving for 100 miles, we could hear the wheel making noise. Johnny said that was the sound of the bearings grinding, and the wheel would come off soon. We all yelled and pounded on the camper walls but they couldn't hear us in the front. Johnny told us we had to stop the truck, or there would be a bad wreck. We opened the

The Story of Two Alaskan Children Growing Up Wild

side window over the little sink and Johnny being the bravest crawled out. Holding onto the top of the camper, he pulled himself along the side of the camper until he could kick the window and get them to see him.

He then worked his way back and crawled back in the window. The driver had started to slow down to about 30 miles per hour when the wheel came off. The truck went off the road and landed mostly on its side. We all got tumbled about in the camper. We were all banged up to some degree. Everything in the cupboards flew out, and we were pelted with dishes and canned goods. Thankfully, no one was seriously hurt. The truck wasn't to banged up either. So Johnny was leaving Alaska a hero once again.

Stella, our sister, got a ride to the next town and called home for help. Someone came from the convent to get me, as it was not too far off. I never saw who came to fix the truck. It did get fixed, and they continued their trip to the lower 48. I was kind of misplaced at first, but soon grew to like it there. There was plenty of food and no wood to chop or haul in. We all had chores, but it was all easy stuff at least compared to my house. All I had to do was learn. What a great and happy time that was. I was soon reading everything in the new library.

I tried out for the ski team and got selected. This

Johnny & Me

allowed me outside a lot more. I loved the ski team. Although I was not the best skier on the team, I held up my part. We went everywhere competing with other schools, always meeting new people and seeing new places. The Catholic school turned out to be a lot better than I had thought it would. My family really never had any contact with me while I was there though.

Father thought it would be better if I made it on my own I guess. I missed everyone but knew they had a hard time just living, and I was fine. Stella did send me a couple of care packages. No letter but jerky, chewing tobacco and fudge, I traded everything but the jerky. The girls from the villages all chewed Copenhagen, so I got some good trading from it. I don't like chocolate, so I was able to get smoked salmon for it. I had quite a stash. My brother John Joe came for me at Christmas. I got to go home for a week. We went ice fishing on one of the lakes near our house. Later, we went caribou hunting, and I filled up on steak. It was a great visit seeing everyone at home. I missed Johnny not being there though.

My winter break went by to quickly, and John Joe took me back to school. I took a cash of trading goods with me. Moose jerky just for me, and snuff and licorice ropes for the girls at school. Trading kept me in dry fish for the rest of

The Story of Two Alaskan Children Growing Up Wild

the year.

It was very cold in Copper Center that winter, as it usually is. Getting down to below 60 degrees at times. It was mostly too cold to go beyond the buildings. We had a giant circle in the middle of the complex under roof, but it was not heated. Instead it was flooded for ice-skating. Everyone got in a lot of skating for exercise. This was something I enjoyed, as skiing was not happening in the cold temperatures. We even had a skating party after midnight mass. We got hot chocolate and cookies from the kitchen on that occasion.

Everyone had chores. I loved when I got chapel duty. It was only if you excelled in class, you were picked for chapel duty. Cleaning the chapel was a special honor. Also you got to serve the priests and sisters in their dinning room. There was no talking in the dinning room.

You had to show up for six o'clock mass to get breakfast, or have a good reason why not. I always got breakfast. I would on occasion go to mass with my nightgown under my coat. I got caught for that after awhile, as I had bare legs and someone noticed. Oh well, that was okay; I just dressed real fast after that. Just wetting my braids and slicking my hair back smooth to save time. I would braid my hair after breakfast and before classes. We

Johnny & Me

had an hour of free time then.

If you went outside with wet hair, you stood a good chance of breaking off your braids. It happened because it was so cold it would freeze solid. One of my roommates had that happen to one of her braids. It broke halfway up her one braid when she slipped on the ice. Her braids were a lot shorter after she had evened out the other braid. I was careful to not go out with damp hair, unless I couldn't avoid it. I would make sure my braids were under my collar and wrapped with a scarf. My braids came through that winter intact.

My lungs were not as lucky. I had family that lived only one mile away and would visit them when I could, walking there and back in what time I was given. On one occasion, I stayed a little too long and only had ten minuets to get back. It was fifty-five below zero, and I ran the mile back. I made it just in time, but I frosted my lungs. I got pneumonia and was sick in bed for a week. Although I got over the pneumonia, my lungs never fully recovered. I've had weak lungs since then.

We got buffalo meat as some one hit a buffalo with a truck near Delta Junction, and the convent was given the meat. That was the only buffalo we ate, but we were given a lot of caribou and moose from road kills. Never enough for

The Story of Two Alaskan Children Growing Up Wild

everyone to have steak, but a lot of roast and stews. We always had a lot of salmon donated too. I don't think we ever had beef. A lot of the meat was ground and used for many different dishes.

Our cook was sister Katherine Mary, and she was a really good cook. We all took turns helping in the kitchen. It was always fun in the kitchen, as sister Katherine was a joy. I didn't mind washing pots and pans, as did some of the girls. After all there was hot water right at the sink and a drain, so you didn't have to haul the water in or out. It was easy work. Sister Katherine liked me and gave me treats sometimes. I was living a life of luxury.

Even with the luxury life, I missed my brother. It would be two years before we were reunited. It was a great learning experience at the convent and life was full of lessons. Learning to act like a lady was the only one I had trouble doing. I did try to please everyone, but I was clumsy and walked like a boy, which is not so great in a dress. Even the book on the head really didn't help much. "Humble, Hilda." "Humble," was repeated, "always portray humble." I bowed my head, but my shoulders said "no." Sister Alice would sigh and shake her head. It just never got better. I was sent to the balcony for mass to diminish my pride. I liked it in the balcony. It was nice up there. Only a few of the sisters would be there. You could see and hear everything, and no one could see you. I started to go there whenever I could, just to be alone and pray by myself. Sometimes just to think. No one ever said anything to me, and it made life a little better for me.

The rest of the time seemed to fly past, and soon it was spring. The fields and meadows were covered with crocuses. White and lavender flowers were everywhere, such a beautiful awakening of summer. Everyone spent as much time outside as we could. Sitting under a tree and smelling the dirt and moss was such a restorative power. I once didn't come back when our free time was over. One of the sisters found me sleeping on the moss under a tree. She just woke me and sent me inside. I wasn't in trouble only told to not do that again. I didn't. It was time to be outside working in the garden getting ready for planting anyway. A lot of my free time would be spent working in the garden. It made me think of home and my family. I am pretty sure I was the most dedicated garden worker they had, although long dresses are not the best for that line of work. The front of my dresses were covered with ground-in dirt. Soon one of the sisters found me some army pants and a belt, which was so much, better for my dresses and me.

If I ever turned up missing, everyone knew where I

The Story of Two Alaskan Children Growing Up Wild

was. I spent every free moment in the garden. There was not one weed in the garden, and not one plant went thirsty. Soon we had fresh radishes and lettuce followed by green onions, peas, and zucchini. It was good to have all the fresh produce. There's nothing like fresh salads with new peas.

Then school was over. Father came and got me to work at home. I was excited to go home, but would miss my big garden. Oh well, we had a garden at home too. There would be plenty to do at home now with Johnny still in Wyoming. It would be lonely without him. We had always worked together. Thankfully, I at least had the horses.

Mother was not there, as she had gone out of state, and father had a new woman. She didn't like me. I was sent to work in the mountain hunting camps by myself. Preparing camps was nothing new, so off I went. I had a couple of dogs and a couple of horses with me, so I guess I wasn't totally alone.

I needed the horses to pull logs and move rocks off the airstrip. The airstrip was a priority, so the supplies could be brought in. The airstrip washed out each spring, as it is on a sandbar in the middle of the river. It always has logs and rocks washed onto it. The logs I dragged to camp and cut up for firewood. The rocks I rolled or dragged back into the river.

Johnny & Me

It was hard work, but it made me sleep well. Some nights, I slept too well. I woke up one morning with the dogs going crazy. A bear was circling the cabin looking for a way in. It was a rather large bear and pretty scary looking. I may have thought it was bigger than it was, as I don't like bears. I had a rifle, but didn't want to wound the bear and make it mad. I just crawled up in the loft where there was a little window. I waited for the bear to come around back again and shot under it to scare it off. That worked! I was a little afraid to work outside on the river that day, so I took the rifle with me and a horse for a quick get away just in case. The bear never came back.

The next camp was only a tent, so not very bear proof. By the time I got there, the bears had shredded the tent and destroyed pretty much everything else. What the bears didn't destroy, the porcupines had chewed up. It was a real mess and took a lot of work to fix everything. Thankfully there was a cache in a tree that wasn't damaged. Had to remake the tent, as even the side poles were broken. It wasn't pretty when I was done, but would keep the rain off. I had another airstrip to clean and drag smooth. At least this one wasn't as bad as the last. When I finished each airstrip, I would put up a wind flag to help the pilots know when they could land.

The Story of Two Alaskan Children Growing Up Wild

I never had any more bear troubles that summer, but I had a lot of squirrel damage and porcupines chewing up everything with salt. Any leather or wood that had touched the horses had salt on them. Any pack boxes left in the camps or horse gear of any kind had gotten chewed.

Porcupines did not care if you were there or not; they would come right into the tent with you. Which is why I spent most of one full day pulling quills out of the two dogs' faces. A porcupine had come into the tent at night, and both dogs attacked it. I think they lost that fight. I guess so did the porcupine. We ate it for dinner. It didn't taste that good, but the dogs liked it. Besides, porcupine was something different from the squirrels we had been eating. We had fish too, but it took more of them to fill the dogs. I had to pick all the bones out of the fish, and some of those fish were small. A plane stopped by one day and brought me some food, even some canned spinach. We had a feast that night. The dogs got the corned beef hash, and I got the spinach. It was all good.

We were off to the next camp. I packed up what we had to take with us on the extra horse. All was well, as we made our way down river. That is until we walked over a ground beehive. My packhorse started bucking and ran over the dogs that were rolling around trying to get the bees off.

Johnny & Me

The packhorse was tailed to my saddle horse, which made her start bucking. I had no place to go, so I grabbed a tree as I passed it. I wound up on the ground under the packhorse and being stung by bees. I rolled away to keep from being trampled and kicked. Unfortunately, the horse did get one good kick to my leg. It gave me a heck of a good bruise.

After we finally got untangled and away from the bees, I had to go back and get everything the packhorse had unloaded. At least the bees had calmed down, and I could see where they were swarming. I stayed away as much as I could. I think I may not have picked up everything, as some things were just too close to the bees. Someone else could get them later. At least the pack boxes had gotten thrown clear, so were easy to retrieve.

I only went a couple miles away and made camp as the packhorse had a lot of bee stings that needed to be covered in salve. When I unsaddled the horse, there were a couple of bees still in the pack boxes. They flew home with no more trouble to us. I needed a bit of salve myself, and my leg was still pretty sore. I limped around camp for a couple days and getting on my horse was no easy task. At least nothing was broken on horse or me, so work continued.

The Story of Two Alaskan Children Growing Up Wild

My last camp was a tent cabin. I just needed to replace the tarp roof. The weight of the winter snow had collapsed the top pole. It was an easy fix. There were plenty of poles to replace it. I put the tarp on and left for home. I had spent over a month in the mountains, so was ready for a turn at home.

When I got back to the homestead I was very pleased to see my friend Harry was there. I was going to have fun after all. He had just come up the day before. Good timing. Father put us to cleaning the saddle shed. All saddles needed to be cleaned, oiled, and hung up, as well as all the other tack. All the pack boxes needed to be checked for damage, so they could be repaired.

After working on that for a while, Harry and I wandered off to the big corral to watch the horses. I decided to catch one of the unbroken ones and saddle it. Harry tried to stop me, but I went in anyway. I did get a rope on one and got dragged all over that pen. That wasn't the worst of it, as I also got run over and kicked. Harry jumped in and got me out. The rope was still on the horse. There was no way to get it off. Of course father knew what happened and who was at fault. I got a few more bruises on my backside from him. I thought I had been punished enough just by the horses. We had to finish the saddle shed too. That took us a couple more days, but we paid attention to what we were supposed to do and didn't cause any more trouble for a while. Well, that wasn't really much trouble anyway, just to me mostly.

I thought I was too old for a butt-whooping. Guess I was wrong. I got a couple more that summer. I always found something to get into. Mostly it didn't cause a problem for anyone but me.

I thought we should make some whiskey, but Harry and I had no idea how. Knowing you were supposed to cook it, we got a big pot and filled it with water and a bag of sugar. We put it on a campfire. As it boiled, we added rhubarb and strawberries. We cooked it for quite a while till it kind of thickened up. Then poured it in jars. After it cooled, we drank some. It didn't get us drunk but tasted good on pancakes. I guess we ended up making syrup. Father was mad at us for taking the sugar and confiscated all our jars.

Harry had to go home after a couple of weeks, so it was back to me being alone again. Father's woman didn't like me any better now than the beginning of summer. I spent the rest of the summer in the mountains until school started again.

I went Eagle River this time. Boarded with an older

The Story of Two Alaskan Children Growing Up Wild

couple whose children had grown up and were on their own. Chugiak High School was my new school. It was a very nice school. My guardians helped me get a job at the school in the library, my favorite place in the world.

I made enough money to buy what I needed, like tooth paste and shampoo. I was even able to save some for Christmas presents. I bought each of my siblings a small gift and sent them in the mail. I don't know if they ever got them, as I never heard from anyone.

I made friends with a few of the kids at school, mostly the troublemakers. We never did anything really wrong, just hung out by the doors and told big lies to each other. We were told to stay out of the doorways as we impeded traffic and to quit sitting on the heaters in the foyers. We did it anyway, because it was warm there.

Some of the boys had snow machines. They took me for rides on them. Whoo-hoo! That was lots of fun. That is until we rolled it down the hill. No one was hurt, except for a few bruises, but it kind of ended our snow machining. At least it was the end for me. I needed to study anyway, as I was getting behind. I caught up my homework quickly, and all was well. I finished my classes and went back to Chickaloon the next spring. I was pretty excited as Johnny was coming home. We had a lot to share. It had been two

Johnny & Me

years after all. We were not little children anymore. We were teenagers. When he came home, I hardly recognized him. Johnny was so tall and all grown up. I hugged him anyway. We were going to be off on even bigger adventures in the future.